50

WAYS TO
IMPROVE
YOUR
NAVIGATION

Published by Adlard Coles Nautical
an imprint of A & C Black Publishers Ltd
38 Soho Square, London, W1D 3HB
www.adlardcoles.com

First edition 2008

ISBN 978-0-7136-8270-0

A CIP catalogue record for this book is
available from the British Library.

This book is produced using paper that is
made from wood grown in managed,
sustainable forests. It is natural, renewable
and recyclable. The logging and
manufacturing processes conform to the
environmental regulations of the country of
origin.

Typeset in 9pt MetaPlusNormal
Printed and bound in China by Wing King Tong

Note: while all reasonable care has been
taken in the publication of this book, the
publisher takes no responsibility for the use
of the methods or products described in the
book.

WAYS TO
IMPROVE
YOUR
NAVIGATION

DAG PIKE

ADLARD COLES NAUTICAL
LONDON

contents

4732245.

WAYS TO IMPROVE YOUR NAVIGATION

contents

ELECTRONIC CHARTS

RADAR FOR NAVIGATION

COLLISION AVOIDANCE

NIGHT AND FOG NAVIGATION

HARBOUR NAVIGATION

1 MAKING A LANDFALL – ANGLE OF APPROACH

MAKING LANDFALL AT AN ANGLE GIVES YOU MORE OPTIONS IF YOU FIND UNEXPECTED SHALLOWS, ALTHOUGH THE RADIO MAST ON THIS HEADLAND MAKES IDENTIFICATION CLEAR.

There are many situations where you come from seaward to make a landfall. It could be after a long open sea passage, it could be coming into an anchorage for lunch or it could be making for harbour. These will be the times when you move from deep water into the shallows and where, if you keep going blindly on, you will hit something or run aground. With GPS operating and the depth sounder running, you should be in control of the situation and the landfall will go according to plan. However, poor visibility or uncertain chart information can raise the risk levels of making a landfall, and things can get critical very quickly.

One way to reduce the risk is to choose the point of landfall carefully. Even if it's not your final destination, you can make

sure you avoid any off-lying dangers and find a point where a gradual shoaling will give you early warning of arrival.

Another way to reduce the risk is to vary the angle of approach. If you are heading straight in towards land and the unexpected happens, you have two options about which way to turn to get out of danger: left or right. There will probably be little or no indication about which is the best way to turn when the sounder shows sudden shoaling or other dangers loom up ahead. But whichever way you decide to go, you will need to make a 180 degree turn before you start to head towards safety.

You can take a lot of the guesswork out of the situation if you approach the land at an angle of around 45 degrees. Not only will this slow down your approach into the shallows and give you more warning of hazards, it will also remove the dilemma about which way to turn if you encounter a problem. If you adopt this angled approach not only is there only one logical way to turn but the turn itself will also be less acute, and you will be able to resolve the situation a lot quicker and a lot more safely.

If you are making a landfall like this under sail, the wind direction will have a considerable bearing on your actions. It may limit your angle of approach in the

6

PREPARATION

first place: you don't want to be close hauled and have to turn up into wind to get out of trouble, as you could lose steerageway at a critical moment. Close-hauled, you will probably have to turn through at least 90 degrees to start

moving away from danger, so consider finding an angle of approach that allows you to change direction both quickly and safely. Under both power and sail, if you have a bow thruster, have this switched on ready for use to speed up the turn.

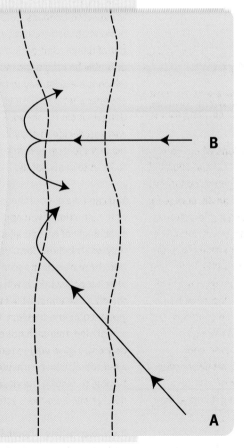

WHEN MAKING A LANDFALL IN POOR VISIBILITY IT IS BETTER TO APPROACH AT THE ANGLE SHOWN IN A. APPROACHING THE COAST DIRECTLY AS IN B MEANS HAVING TO TURN THROUGH A GREATER ANGLE IF YOU DETECT SUDDEN SHOALING AND YOU WON'T NECESSARILY KNOW WHICH IS THE SAFEST WAY TO TURN.

2 DEVIATING TO SHORTEN THE DISTANCE BETWEEN MARKS

WHEN YOU PLAN YOUR ROUTE TO PASS CLOSE TO A BUOY IT NOT ONLY SHORTENS THE VISUAL DISTANCE BETWEEN MARKS, IT CAN ALSO GIVE YOU A CHECK ON WHAT THE TIDE IS DOING.

Normally when you want to travel between two points you will draw a direct line on the chart to give the shortest distance. However, when you plot this shortest route it may not be ideal from a navigation point of view, so you should look at other possibilities before finalising it. You also need to check the route to ensure that you aren't proposing something that takes you over or close to navigation hazards but there can also be other considerations to take into account.

If you are navigating using GPS position fixing on an electronic chart, the direct route should work because you are getting constant fixes along the way. However, it is always prudent to check your position using sources other than GPS. You can easily do this by making minor modifications to your route. Look along your proposed route and seek out navigation marks (such as buoys marking isolated shoals or rocks) that lie on either side of it. It may be sufficient to just see them in the distance but in poor visibility you might want to deviate from the straight-line course to get a positive fix.

If you do decide to deviate from the course in order to pass closer to these marks you obviously need to pass on the safe side of the buoy, away from the danger that they mark. If you follow this method of visual checks, you could end up with something of a zigzag course, but unless you have made major deviations the actual distance is not likely to be much greater than the straight line.

The benefit of adopting this tactic is that you will get regular visual checks on your position as you go along. These not only offer reassurance but also provide a check on the performance of the GPS.

Whilst GPS is very reliable and will rarely let you down, one of the golden rules of safe navigation is to check your position from at least two independent sources.

Making regular visual checks does this in a very positive way and it also allows you to see what the tide is doing when you pass the buoy.

DEVIATING TO GET A FIX WHEN MAKING A LANDFALL CAN BE VERY HELPFUL IN FOG.

3 THE LONGER ROUTE CAN BE THE QUICKEST

If you are crossing a bay and going into head seas, the direct route from headland to headland may not be the quickest. It can often pay to deviate into the bay and follow the coastline around to the next headland (provided of course that there are no navigation hazards that could cause a danger on the way). The tactics will differ between powerboats and sailboats but there are benefits for both.

There are several advantages to taking the longer route. Firstly, by altering course into the bay you will be putting the wind on the bow instead of directly ahead. In a powerboat, this should give you a more comfortable ride. Secondly, as you head into the bay you will start to receive protection from the worst of the seas by the headland that lies on the other side. This means that when you have to turn along the coastline and head into the wind, you should find better sea conditions and get a better ride, allowing an increase in speed.

Conditions should continue to improve as you approach the next headland, allowing a faster and smoother ride. By doing this, the trip around the bay should be quicker than the trip directly across, and you will get a more comfortable ride into the bargain. You will still have to face the head seas when you reach the headland but you can

often find a patch of relatively smooth water close in under the headland where the tides are weaker. Check the chart closely before going close around the headland to make sure there are no rocks or shallows close in that could cause danger. Also be aware of any tide races that might exist, where both the tides and the wind can be stronger.

On a sailboat, when there is a headwind from headland to headland, you will be faced with the option of tacking into the bay or tacking out to seaward. Whilst the inshore option may look attractive because it takes you out of the rough seas and the possibly stronger adverse tide, you may find that the wind is heading you along the coastline as you come out of the bay. If this happens, you will need to tack out again at a fairly early stage in order to round the headland safely.

The benefits of this tactic will depend a great deal on the topography of the bay and you may not find any great advantage if the bay has only a slight indentation between the headlands. The best conditions for this tactic are more likely to be found in a deep bay with pronounced headlands where there will be good shelter under the lee of the land. Always check the chart carefully to make sure that you have safe waters on the projected inside course.

THE EFFECT OF WIND ON THE TIDES

At first glace there does not appear to be any reason why the wind should affect the tide but it does so in two ways. Firstly it can affect the strength of the tidal flow and secondly, it can affect the height of the tide. And of course, as in most situations where the wind is involved, the stronger the wind is, the more noticeable the effects will be.

The tidal stream is a mass of flowing water, strongest in the middle of the stream but slowed at the edges where it comes into contact with shallower water or land. As the wind is in direct contact with the surface of the flowing water it is not hard to picture the effect. When the wind is blowing with the tide, the tidal stream will flow stronger at the surface and the effect will be felt a metre or so down. This top layer of water is the region where boats operate, so the stronger tidal flow will directly affect your progress.

Secondly, there will be an effect on the height of the tide. This is caused partly because the increase in the tidal flow can result in a surge, with the tide flowing when the wind and tide are in the same direction. Equally, when the wind and tide are in opposition the outgoing water flow will be held up and its height will be maintained. These surging and holding back effects are most apparent when strong winds have been blowing from the same direction for some time. Strong winds within 100 miles or more can still affect the tides in your area of water.

Wind

Sheltered water

IT IS OFTEN FASTER, AND CERTAINLY MORE COMFORTABLE, TO DEVIATE INTO A BAY TO GET PROTECTION FROM WIND AND SEA. A SAILBOAT WOULD HAVE TO TACK ANYWAY, BUT A POWERBOAT CAN OFTEN MAKE A QUICKER PASSAGE BY TAKING THE LONGER INSHORE ROUTE.

THE SEA CONDITIONS HERE ARE VERY GENTLE, BUT COULD EASILY WORSEN IF THE TIDE TURNS IN OPPOSITION TO THE WIND.

5 JUDGING SEA CONDITIONS

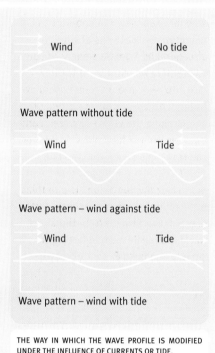

Wave pattern without tide

Wave pattern – wind against tide

Wave pattern – wind with tide

THE WAY IN WHICH THE WAVE PROFILE IS MODIFIED UNDER THE INFLUENCE OF CURRENTS OR TIDE.

When you are planning a passage it's not just the route that concerns you; you also want to know what the sea conditions will be like. This can be particularly important for powerboats, where the prevailing sea conditions can have a significant impact on performance, but sailboats would normally be looking for a comfortable ride as well.

Obviously, you can get a general idea of what to expect from the weather forecast, and experience will tell you which sea conditions are associated with different wind strengths. However, there can be localised areas where the seas get worse and identifying these can be critical to making a safe and comfortable passage.

There are two main factors that can cause sea conditions to deteriorate beyond what would normally be expected from the forecast, and these are the winds and the tides. As far as the wind is concerned, you can find areas where the wind strength could increase beyond what the forecast suggests. This mainly occurs when the wind is funnelled through narrow channels or around high headlands. As the wind is forced to deviate from a straight line, it is being compressed, which increases the strength by one or two numbers on the Beaufort scale. In both of these situations the increase in the strength of the wind can lead to rougher seas.

As far as the tides are concerned, you will usually find steeper and higher waves in areas where the wind is flowing against the tide. In these wind-against-tide conditions, the wavelength tends to be reduced, and this will generate uncomfortable sea conditions for both power and sailing yachts. Just like the wind, the tide will also tend to be stronger where it is forced through narrow channels and around headlands so expect to find worse sea conditions in those places. You should also watch out for tidal races in these areas; localised areas of steep breaking waves are particularly prevalent when the wind is against the tide. The chart will often identify the worst of these potential conditions but in other areas it is up to you to assess the effects of the wind and tide on the sea conditions.

There is no hard and fast rule that will enable you to predict the conditions accurately, but if you remember that wind against tide will produce shorter, steeper seas then you should be able to picture the patterns of wind direction and tidal flow and work out where they will conflict. A further factor to take into account is shallow water, which will have the effect of encouraging the waves to break earlier than they might have done in deeper water.

Predicting the conditions is one thing but avoiding them is another, so you may want to deviate from the direct route in the interests of finding a smoother passage.

THE SEAS ARE ROUGH BUT BECAUSE THE FETCH IS SHORT THE WAVES ARE NOT HIGH.

OFFSETTING THE COURSE IN ORDER TO BE SURE

OFFSETTING THE COURSE CAN HELP YOU MAKE A POSITIVE LANDFALL.

When planning a passage, it might seem logical to draw a straight line on the electronic or paper chart to link up the departure and arrival points, but think ahead a little and consider the options. Think about the situation and what might happen if the visibility closes in and you don't find what you are looking for on arrival. If you are making a landfall on a featureless coastline, will you know which way to turn if you don't find the land features that you expected?

The accuracy of the GPS should take any of the guesswork out of the

situation, but what do you do if something goes wrong? If at the end of a long passage you sight land and cannot recognise any of the features, you will have the choice of turning left or right to locate your destination. If you originally set the course directly for your destination, you won't know which way to turn.

One way of avoiding this dilemma is to build an offset into the course that you steer from the word go. Rather than following a direct line between departure and arrival points, offset the course by around 5°. It doesn't particularly matter which way you build in this offset, provided the new course does not take you close to any dangers. On a sailboat you will also need to consider the direction of the wind and tide when deciding on the offset because you don't want to end up having to fight one or other at the end of the passage in order to get to your destination. The point is that you know you won't arrive at your chosen destination but you will definitely arrive to one side of it.

This offsetting technique is probably going to be most useful when you are making for a harbour entrance that has little in the way of distinguishing features until you get close. Then, the offset will allow you to run along the coast it to find the entrance you are looking for. This is a technique that should be used selectively and it may not prove to be a good solution when finding a harbour where shallow water extends some way offshore. This could create more problems that it solves. But even in this age of GPS plotting, offsetting your course can be a useful technique to have up your sleeve.

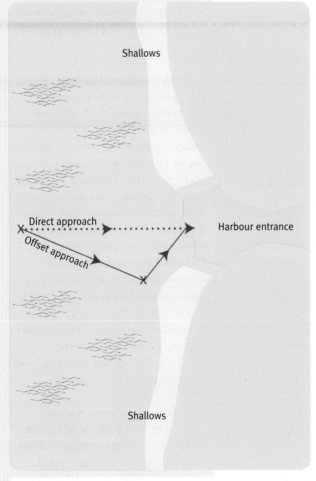

Shallows

Direct approach

Harbour entrance

Offset approach

Shallows

THE DIRECT APPROACH MAY NOT ALWAYS BE THE BEST.

7 SAFETY MARGINS

GPS can be dangerous. By offering you constant position fixing (so that in theory you always know where you are) it can encourage you to cut corners. With GPS positioning, there is no obvious reason why you shouldn't plot your course close to sandbanks and rocks. When you know where you are with an accuracy that can be measured in metres, you feel in full control of the navigation situation.

Traditionally, navigators have always allowed wide safety margins because of relatively poor position accuracy. This cautious approach also allowed a margin for unforeseen tidal and wind influences, or gear or engine failures. Whilst using GPS, your boat is still affected by unforeseen influences, and you need to remember that the electronic chart is only plotting your position – it is not correcting the course and maintaining the course-line unless you set this facility up. You will only become aware of approaching danger if you watch the plotter at all times, so you can detect any drift inshore towards the rocks or other dangers.

In normal circumstances, you are unlikely to be constantly monitoring the electronic chart, so it makes sense to allow safety margins when you plan your route. Yes, you may want to pass close to a buoy to confirm your position, and that's fine because the buoy will be laid some distance from the danger it's marking. However take care when you do this, because several other boats may have the same idea. One effect of GPS navigation is the way that boats now tend to congregate around marks because they're all using the same waypoint, and you can unexpectedly find yourself in congested waters.

You also need to be prepared for the possibility of a breakdown or system failure. Perhaps the autopilot will fail but you don't hear the alarm for a while. Maybe the steering or the GPS will break down. A temporary engine failure could leave you drifting. These are all rare occurrences but you will thank yourself if you have allowed an adequate safety margin that gives you time to cope. At night, you need to allow a bigger margin, because you have a decreased sensory awareness of your position.

These safety margins normally just mean allowing a reasonable distance off dangers or turning marks. They are unlikely to add a great deal to the distance you travel, but can add considerably to your peace of mind.

FUEL AND NAVIGATION

Fuel is a finite resource at sea and when you are planning your passage it can prove a critical factor. Although this applies more to power craft than sailing boats, the fuel left, and thus the range available can be an important factor to consider on both types of craft. If things don't turn out as planned, your fuel supply can dictate your tactics.

The key with fuel is to never let it get so low that it closes down your options and your tactics. If you plan to reach a harbour that is close to the limits of your fuel range this can severely limit your options at the end of your journey, and you will have little choice but to enter the harbour, whether or not the conditions are safe to do so. As most yachts use their engines to enter harbour this is just as important for sail as it is for power. Indeed, adequate fuel is often more important for sailboats because if the wind drops they can be forced to use their engines more than they had expected.

When planning a passage there should therefore be adequate fuel on board not only to reach the chosen port but also to divert to an alternative port if necessary. This alternative port may be nearer or further than the destination port, but wherever it is, make sure you check out any tidal or other entry limitations. As a rough estimate you should always aim

to be safely in harbour with at least 15% of your fuel left. If fog comes down or there is unexpected bad weather you may have to seriously reappraise your tactics. It's worth remembering that a boat is likely to use more fuel when operating in rough seas, so a good fuel margin can be a very important part of your navigation planning.

WHEN YOU REFUEL BEFORE A PASSAGE ENSURE THAT YOU HAVE ADEQUATE FUEL TO REACH AN ALTERNATIVE PORT IF NECESSARY.

ADDING UP THE CLUES

With visual navigation, you are never likely to be 100% sure of your position unless you are close to a buoy or other fixed marker. However, total accuracy does not matter in most situations and knowing your position within half a mile or so will often suffice even when you are navigating along a coastline. Sometimes it can be just as important to know where you are not as to know where you are. And there are many clues out there that can help you. On its own, each clue might not seem too important, but when you add them together you can get a good impression of whether you are on track or moving into danger.

Out in the open sea and away from land, the only visual clues you are likely to get are from soundings. A deep or relatively shallow area can often give you an indication of your position and your echo sounder is one of the most useful tools for visual navigation. The depth can also indicate where you are not, and either way, it is useful information.

Closer to land, there are many more positional clues in addition to the navigation marks and soundings. For example, two identifiable marks on the shore in line (or nearly in line) will give you a position line and you must be somewhere along it. A single mark can help you fix your position if it lies ahead (or nearly ahead) and again you know

that you are somewhere along that heading line.

One of the biggest assets in visual navigation is the ability to judge distances at sea. If you have a bearing or a heading and you can judge your distance off it, you have a fix of sorts. Even ferries operating on a fixed route can give a guide to your position, although this should be done with considerable caution.

There are so many visual clues out there if you know what to look for. The changing patterns of waves can indicate a shoal area or tide race. Clouds seen near the horizon can indicate that there is land in the distance. It is by combining some or all of these clues that you can form a pretty good idea of where you are, and this can be a useful check even if you are using GPS. Having a good awareness of your surroundings and relating what you see outside to what is shown on the chart – that is an important part of navigation. If you understand these ideas then you will be less likely to panic if you get some form of electronic failure on board. By using the visual clues around you, you should be able to find your way to land and a safe harbour.

THERE CAN BE MANY CLUES TO YOUR POSITION FROM THE COASTLINE, USING BUILDINGS, MOUNTAINS AND OTHER FEATURES IN ADDITION TO THE MAIN NAVIGATION MARKS.

10 POSITION FIXING FROM SEA CONDITIONS

ROUGH SEAS LIKE THESE OFF A HEADLAND CAN GIVE AN INDICATION OF POSITION IN POOR VISIBILITY.

It may sound an unlikely way to find your position, but changes in sea conditions are often clues to where you are. Waves at sea are rarely regular and they change their shape and pattern for a variety of reasons. Shallow water, rocks, currents, tidal streams and even the topography of the land can all have their effect on the size and shape of waves, and these changes will provide a useful position guide if you understand why they occur and how they happen.

Shallow water and rocks are obviously something you want to avoid and the breaking seas on these features will give you both a warning and an indication of where you are. Beware, though, that shallow water will not always produce breaking waves in calm seas. In fact, unless the water is very shallow you are unlikely to see breaking waves if they

are under one metre high. Also, if you are viewing them from seaward, which is most likely, they might not be as clearly visible as they would be from the other direction. Breaking seas on rocks are likely to be much more localised but again, they won't always be clearly visible from seaward and if there's a big sea running, they may be lost in the general breaking wave crests associated with the strong wind.

When you want to locate areas of shallow water, for example over extensive shoals where the navigation marks may be few and far between, a low swell in the open sea will give you the best type of conditions for this. This swell will rise up when it encounters the shallow water and is much more likely to produce breaking waves than the wind, and they will also be much more visible.

Strong tides and currents will often produce breaking seas and these will be more evident when the wind is blowing against the current. This type of wave is quite distinctive – there can be standing waves that break continuously in one place when there are strong currents. They may be marked on charts if they are a regular occurrence, and you are more likely to find them where the tidal flow is constricted (such as around headlands or in narrow channels). These are normally places best avoided, as the waves can be quite dangerous, but from a distance they can give a useful

indication of position. The topography of the land will suggest where currents and tides might be constricted to produce breaking seas, and the tidal atlas will show you where the currents are running strongly.

Breaking waves provide valuable clues about your position but you need to be very aware that they often represent dangers. They act more as a navigation warning than as an absolute position check so you should look at these possibilities in your route planning, to be sure they don't take you by surprise.

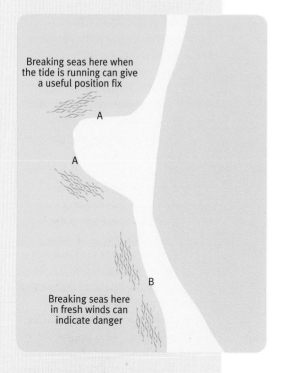

Breaking seas here when the tide is running can give a useful position fix

A

A

B

Breaking seas here in fresh winds can indicate danger

11 ESTIMATING YOUR POSITION

If you don't have the precision of GPS, you will rarely be able to know exactly where your boat is. You can pick up visual pointers; the depth can help and bearings will add to the mix of clues. Nothing will be precise but at least you should be able to form a good estimate of your position and narrow it down to a fairly tight area of possibility. You can still use compass bearings for fixing the position but even then there can be an area of uncertainty.

When making a landfall without GPS you will have had to estimate the effects of winds and tides and you cannot be certain of the exact course that has been steered (see 13: Steering bias) or the speed that you have made good. Here you need to estimate a worst case scenario, adding up all the possible errors so that you end up with a circle or oval of uncertainty. The size of this area of uncertainty will be determined in one direction by possible speed errors and in the other by possible course errors (see diagram). You can be fairly confident that your boat lies somewhere inside it when making your landfall. This area of uncertainty can act as a warning but it's time to start focusing on obtaining information from other sources such as visual sightings and soundings.

What you need to do when making a landfall with a large area of uncertainty

is to try to reduce the size of the area as much as possible. One way to do this is by using a depth check. This will be particularly valuable if the area extends into shallow water – if the sounder shows deep water you know that you're not in the shallow sector and that could reduce your area of uncertainty considerably.

If the landfall is focused on finding a buoy, estimating this circle of uncertainty can be very valuable because it will show the earliest and latest points at which you might see the buoy and the possible directions in which it might lie. Once again, soundings can narrow down the size of your possible area.

Estimating your position is as much about knowing where you can't be as where you could be. If the sounder shows a certain depth then you cannot be in deeper or shallower water (as long as you make allowance for the rise and fall of the tide, if this is significant). Always allow a degree of latitude when using soundings in this way because you are unlikely to get pinpoint accuracy and the chart sounding may not reflect what is actually there. Consider the soundings as a guide rather than an absolute fix.

When you get within sight of land and are lucky enough to get a transit bearing, you know very precisely that your position must lie somewhere along that line. If you see a ferry on a fixed route, you should be somewhere along it. Nothing is certain but all these clues narrow down the area of uncertainty when estimating your position.

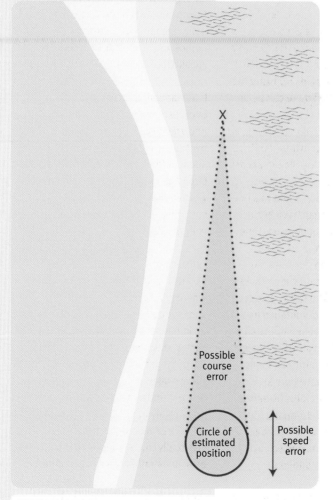

X

Possible course error

Circle of estimated position

Possible speed error

HOW COURSE AND SPEED ERRORS CAN AFFECT YOUR ESTIMATED POSITION.

12 TRANSIT BEARINGS

Transit bearings are one of the best types of position fixing you can have when using visual navigation. Getting two marks in line will give you the most accurate visual indication of where you are, in at least one direction. These transit marks will only give you a position line, but when the marks are aligned you know that your position must lie somewhere along it. You won't know the distance off and you may have to rely on soundings or other clues to fine-tune the position, but you will have narrowed down the options.

When you travel along a coastline you may see a lot of marks that have potential for transit bearings but this is not much use unless the two marks are shown on the chart.

Finding suitable marks isn't always easy. When planning your route look out for conspicuous buildings and other features that are shown on the chart, so you can be prepared for them as you approach. We tend to focus on things like church spires, lighthouses and high buildings but you can extend the range to include distinctive hills and mountains in the distance (provided they are marked on the chart).

One of the best transit marks is a beacon or light on an isolated rock offshore, because its apparent movement will change quite quickly in relation to the background land. Using a buoy as one of the transit marks will widen the scope of possibilities but remember that its position is never exactly as shown on the chart because there has to be some slack in the mooring chain that fixes it to the seabed. Be aware that in this case the transit bearing could be several degrees in error (so you will have a narrow triangle as a position line). Also be wary of using two transit marks quite close together. Here, a small change in the alignment of the marks can produce a large change in the bearing and the accuracy will be reduced.

A TRANSIT BEARING SUCH AS THIS BEACON NEARLY IN LINE WITH THE DISTANT MAST CAN BE A GOOD POSITION INDICATOR PROVIDED THEY ARE BOTH MARKED ON THE CHART.

When steering a compass course it is normal to assume that the person on the helm is steering the required course. You might expect them to wander 5/10° to either side of the required course (and even more in rough weather) but you assume that these swings will average out.

In practice this is rarely the case, and most helmsmen will bias the course to one side or the other. There can be many reasons for this. In a sailboat that is sailing close-hauled, the course is more likely to be dictated by the wind direction than the compass heading, but even when reaching the tendency will be to let the boat wander more off the wind than up into the wind because that is the easy option for the helmsman. When running downwind, the cautious helmsman's course is more likely to be away from the gybe point than towards it.

Under power, the tendency will be much the same, with the bias tending towards the downwind side of the required course rather than heading up into the wind because that is the easier option for the helmsman.

These are all natural reactions for the helmsman, who is probably totally unaware that he isn't steering the required course. However the resulting course can be 5° or more away from the one you actually wanted and this can add up to a considerable error over a distance. You need to take this into account when calculating a dead-reckoning position and the only way to do this is to watch the heading being steered over a period of time.

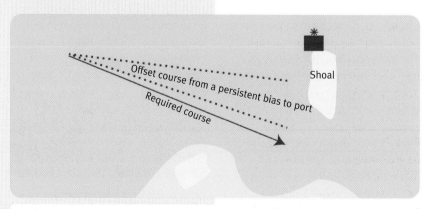

MANY HELMSMEN WILL STEER A COURSE TO ONE SIDE OR THE OTHER OF THE DESIRED COURSE. IT PAYS TO WATCH THE STEERING SO THAT YOU CAN COMPENSATE FOR THE STEERING BIAS ERROR.

14 MAGNETIC OR TRUE?

There was a time when courses and bearings used for steering and position fixing were well organised. Everything was done in magnetic because it all revolved around the magnetic compass (except when it came to transferring courses and bearings onto the paper chart where true courses and bearings were used). On today's boats, the situation with magnetic or true bearings and courses is much more complex, and this can lead to errors unless you develop your own system designed to remove any doubt between the use of magnetic and true.

Paper charts still use true bearings and courses because that is the way they are arranged, but you can use the inner ring on the compass rose to get magnetic readings. Electronic charts work in much the same way, but here everything is a true reading because you don't have a compass rose and there is no toleration in the system for the use of magnetic bearings or courses. The chart is normally north up but although it is possible to vary this all readings are still in true.

Radar is more complex because you can have a North Up or relative display. You may want North Up if you are doing a direct comparison with the electronic chart but most users prefer a relative display with the ship's head at the top of the screen and the picture relating to what you see ahead. If you are using 'ship's head up' and steering a compass course you will be relating any bearing you see or take from the radar as magnetic bearings, and they may need correcting accordingly.

Now we come to the compass itself. Most boats still have a magnetic compass but many also have an electronic compass. Electronic compasses are still based on magnetic readings but the software also gives you the option of having the readout in magnetic or true by automatically applying corrections. Then there are the modern GPS compasses which give a true reading in the same way that a gyrocompass will. With all these options it is easy to see how confusion can occur and you can find yourself steering a course ten degrees or more from the one you want. This situation becomes even more complex because in many cases these days the corrections for converting magnetic to true course can be done automatically.

To avoid mistakes you need to develop a system to use, and in view of the trend towards electronic systems reading in or using true headings, it makes sense to use true readings for everything. This means that the only times you need to convert to magnetic are when you are steering using the magnetic compass or using a hand-bearing compass. Even the latter tend to be electronic these days (and can give true readings) so stick with these and set all the electronics to use true readings, but do understand clearly when you need to switch to magnetic.

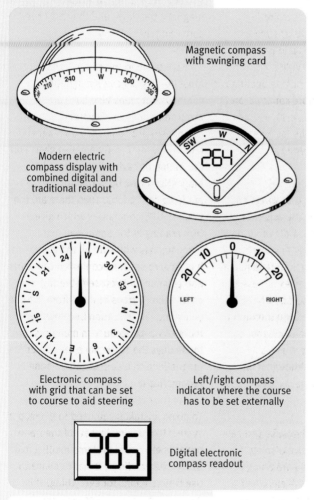

Magnetic compass with swinging card

Modern electric compass display with combined digital and traditional readout

Electronic compass with grid that can be set to course to aid steering

Left/right compass indicator where the course has to be set externally

Digital electronic compass readout

ALTERNATIVE TYPES OF COMPASS DISPLAYS.

15 SECOND STAGE NAVIGATION

FINDING THE BEACON CAN HELP TO IDENTIFY THE LAND BEHIND.

If everything goes according to plan – you run the required course and distance and the mark or land that you were looking for turns up at the end of the run – then you are in control of the navigation. In good visibility you should be able to see what you were looking for even if you end up some way off it. However, if you are way out and can't find what you are looking for, or if the visibility is poor, then second stage navigation can help you sort out the problem.

If you leave things until the problem arises and you don't know where you are, it can be much more difficult to sort out. It's much better to set out a strategy when you are planning the route (the techniques described in 6: Offsetting the course in order to be sure can help). One form of second stage navigation is knowing which way to turn to find what you are looking for. Another possibility is to find the land at the earliest possible moment, even if the point where you make the landfall is not where you were heading for, and then complete the route along the coastline. Not only will this reduce the possible errors in the dead reckoning (the shorter the distance travelled the smaller the errors will be) but it can also allow you to get familiar with the land and identify features before trying to find that elusive harbour entrance. Navigating along a coastline gives you many more clues about your position than being in the open sea away from land.

Another form of second stage navigation entails trying to imagine what the landfall might look like. If you have a mental picture of what you expect to see

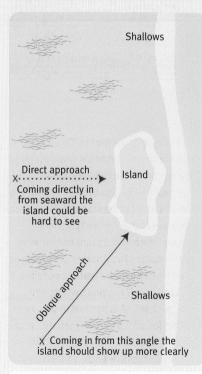

Shallows

Direct approach
X ···············▶ Island
Coming directly in
from seaward the
island could be
hard to see

Oblique approach

Shallows

X Coming in from this angle the
island should show up more clearly

AN ISLAND AGAINST THE LAND CAN BE HARD TO
IDENTIFY.

when you make the landfall this will help you to find an approach where things are clearer and easier to identify. Trying to find a flashing buoy light against a background of bright shore lights can be difficult. Trying to find an island lying against the land can be tricky because in neither case will the target stand out against the background. When you plan your route, think about whether a different angle of approach might make the situation clearer.

Tides and wind are another consideration in second stage navigation. You don't want to be making a landfall or even have the possibility of making a landfall down-tide or downwind from your destination and then have to struggle against these factors to get to the harbour you want to find. You need to think about what lies ahead when planning, and weigh up all the scenarios and options. That deviation you might take in order to make an early landfall could enable you to pick up a stronger inshore tide to help you on your way. Although the distance is greater, this could actually shorten the time.

Second stage navigation is all about thinking ahead, having a plan if you don't find what you are looking for and trying to maintain control of the situation at all times.

16 CONSPICUOUS MARKS

CONSPICUOUS MARKS CAN PROVIDE A REASSURING CHECK ON YOUR NAVIGATION.

When you cruise along a coastline you will see many features that stand out can be clearly identified. In the days when you used a hand-bearing compass to fix your position with bearings, these conspicuous marks were invaluable because they provided the key to knowing where you were. Today it's rare to fix your position with bearings but the conspicuous marks along the coast can still be valuable, because they provide strong clues about where you are.

As we saw in 12: Transit bearings, a conspicuous mark is only really valuable when it is also marked on the chart. Marks may be identified by being annotated 'Spire conspic' or 'tall building conspic'. That was fine when the survey from which the chart was generated was up-to-date but today

many of these so-called conspicuous objects can be either difficult to see or may be confusing.

A church spire may be hidden from view from seaward by tall buildings that have been erected in front of it, and a single tall building when the survey was carried out may now be surrounded by several tall buildings – this can present a confusing picture. There are also some more modern conspicuous marks such as TV masts that have appeared on charts, largely because they have flashing aircraft warning lights on them and can provide a useful guide at night.

There are three main ways in which you can use conspicuous marks. The first is simply as a check on the position – even when using GPS it's reassuring to be able to monitor your progress by using features on the land. If you note when the conspicuous mark is abeam and you know your course, you will have a fairly accurate position line extending at right angles from your course line to the conspicuous mark.

The second way to use the marks is as a steering reference. Steering a compass course can be tedious and takes your focus away from what is going on outside the boat. If you set

the course initially by compass and there is land ahead, try to identify a mark on or near the required heading, as it can provide a much better temporary heading reference to steer by. You will find this much easier than looking at the compass all the time and you are more likely to steer a reasonable course.

Finally, you can use a similar technique to find a harbour entrance. Harbour entrances don't always show up well when you are some way off and if they are located on an otherwise featureless coastline it can be quite confusing. There is usually a town located at a harbour entrance and this will give you a clue to the true location. However if there is a conspicuous mark located nearby, this can be used as a guide to head in the right direction until you can pick out the detail of the entrance.

One use of conspicuous marks that doesn't need them to be shown on the chart is when you are at anchor. Once settled in the anchorage pick out a couple of marks on the shore that are in line – it could be a tree and a house or similar, but they should be on your beam – so that if the anchor drags you will see the marks drift apart and get early warning of the problem. You may need different marks when the tide turns or eases.

THE CHURCH SPIRE COULD MAKE A GOOD STEERING REFERENCE WHEN SEARCHING FOR THE BUOY.

It always sounds like a good idea when someone on board says, 'I know this harbour, let me take over and show you the way in'. It seems like a great way to save you concentrating on trying to find your way into a strange harbour. It's so easy to hand over the navigation in this way but whilst you think you may be handing over the navigation you are not handing over the responsibility. If anything goes wrong it is still your problem.

Handing over the navigation to someone who says they know the area is fine, and you can also learn from what is going on if the volunteer really knows their business. If you are going into a harbour that is new to you, local knowledge can be a great help but you should still make your own plans (study the way in, and look at the marks and channels) so that you also have a good idea of what to expect. If the crew member with the local knowledge does take over you can still learn from what they are doing but, more importantly, you will still be able to take over if things don't work out as expected.

The problem you face as skipper when someone on board offers local knowledge is that you don't know the extent of their knowledge. Local knowledge may cover knowing what the harbour looks like but it may not always extend to knowing depths of water and tides and similar requirements. It may not extend to knowing which VHF radio frequencies to use and where visitors' berths might be found. It's important for you to judge whether your local knowledge person really does know the harbour and its channels, and you can only make that judgement if you have done your own preparation and have a pretty fair idea of the area yourself.

Having an offer of local knowledge can put you in a dilemma and it needs diplomacy on your part to sort it out. The best solution is to let the person advise you but not take over completely, so you remain in control. If there is any conflict between their advice and what you think about the situation, then this is the time to stop if you can and work things out before going any further.

So treat local knowledge with caution. It can be useful to have someone on board who knows what things look like in a strange harbour, but you have to ask whether they have actually navigated a boat like yours in that harbour. They may be used to a dinghy when your draft is two metres. Local knowledge means different things to different people and you would be very unwise to use it as a substitute for doing your normal research about the place you are visiting. Try to remain in control of the situation.

LOCAL KNOWLEDGE COULD BE A GREAT HELP IN NEGOTIATING AN ESTUARY LIKE THIS BUT MAKE SURE THAT THE PERSON WITH THE LOCAL KNOWLEDGE REALLY KNOWS WHAT HE IS DOING.

18 CHECKING THE PLOTTED COURSE

You have drawn the lines on the chart for your required route, passing around headlands and through the required waypoints, and it all looks fine. This is now the time to look much more carefully at the route that you have selected, partly to check that it is safe and partly to look at a variety of options that might be open to you. You will probably have done your initial route planning on a general chart, or if using electronics, on a chart scale that may cover a great deal of the route. Now you need to transfer it to the more detailed charts on a smaller scale so you can see the detail along the route.

The first thing is to check the route for safety. Have you left sufficient margins around dangers in case things don't work out as planned? Are there any dangers along the route that you might have missed when you drew the lines on the chart and do you want to highlight any dangers close to the route (see 31: Waypoint selection and use)? It is surprising how much of the detail is left out of the main route planning charts but which shows up on the large scale charts, so you need to look at the proposed route in the large scale to make sure it's OK. When you are fully satisfied that the route is suitable you can start to look for possible options.

Look for conspicuous objects along the coast that may help you to identify features and places. As detailed in 16: Conspicuous marks, they can also be used as a steering mark if there happens to be land ahead along your chosen route. Look for possible transit bearings that could give you a position line for checking your progress. Look for significant changes in soundings that could help to give you a fix when you keep your sounder on. You can discover so many clues from a close study of the chart that it's worth spending some time doing this.

Once you have extracted all the possible information along the route and have built up a mental picture of where you are proposing to go, it's time to look at some of the more practical aspects. Look to see how the tides will be running and whether they could set you in towards danger. Check whether there are diversions that allow you to miss some of the strongest adverse tides. See what the weather forecast says, assess how it might affect your progress and whether you could find better shelter from a modified route. Under sail, you will also need to look out for wind changes and consider how they will affect things. Under power, you might want to watch out for difficult wind against tide situations around headlands. Check for alternative ports that might be available if the need arises.

Time spent working with the chart, fine-tuning the route, is never wasted. Try to build up a mental picture of what you will expect to see along the route and what the conditions will be like. In this way you can prepare for most eventualities and have strategies to cope with them. Customising the chart (as detailed in the following chapter) can help with this process, enabling you to see things at a quick glance if you are under pressure.

The initial course

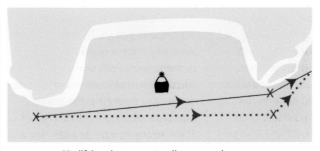

Modifying the course to allow more clearance

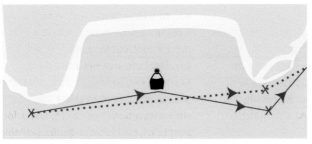

Second modification to pass close to the buoy

19 CUSTOMISING THE CHARTS

A CUSTOMISED CHART ON A RACING BOAT. THIS IS AN EXTREME CASE OF CUSTOMISING BUT IT CAN BE A GREAT HELP IF YOU HIGHLIGHT BUOYS, MARKS AND COURSES, PARTICULARLY WHEN NAVIGATING AT NIGHT.

Paper charts have a huge amount of information on them and there is so much detail included that you often have to study them quite closely to see what is there. Spread out on a table when you are planning the route it can all look fine and easy but in the confines of a yacht chart table and when the boat is moving about at sea, the detail is rarely as clear as you would like it to be. The chart designers have to include a huge amount of information on the chart, so the size is inevitably condensed, and features that look clear in the harsh light of harbour may be less easy to read at night on a stormy sea. The different colours for soundings can be very useful in giving you a general picture but features like isolated dangers and even buoys may not be clear when you are navigating out at sea.

To help clarify things, customising the chart can be a good idea, as you can make sure that the features in which you are particularly interested stand out. Obviously you will have drawn in the routes to be followed and these can be identified with the courses and distances written alongside. A longer course across a wide bay could be marked every five miles or so, so you can do a mental calculation about progress along that leg without having to measure things off.

Buoys and other marks can be highlighted by circling them and if you are navigating at night it's useful to write down the characteristics of the light so you don't need to look at the small print on the chart. Similarly, conspicuous objects (particularly if they are close to the heading you will be steering) are a good feature to identify, and isolated dangers and shoals should also be highlighted, perhaps by colouring or shading. If you are on a sailboat you might want to highlight the inshore depths that are the limit for the inshore course of the tack. By adding in all this detail you have changed the chart into a display that is tailored to your particular navigation requirements.

If you are using the chart for a one-off route, the highlighting and notes on it can be done in pencil. However if you use the area frequently and tend to follow the same courses, you can make more permanent changes by using highlighter pens and different colours for buoys and lights. It can be a good idea in any case to mark a variety of possible courses on the chart so you have readily available alternatives when you are at sea. It is also a good idea to make a note of the tide times, particularly the times at which the tidal flow is expected to change. With all this customising on the chart, you now have virtually all the navigation information you need in one place, ready for instant use. This can be particularly valuable on a faster powerboat where using instruments on the chart can be very difficult, if not impossible.

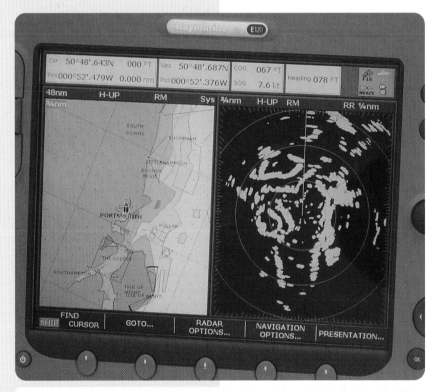

YOU ARE VERY LIMITED IN THE WAYS IN WHICH YOU CAN CUSTOMISE THE ELECTRONIC CHART.

20 USING POSITION LINES

There are many different position lines that are useful for navigation but they all have one thing in common. A position line is a line that has been determined on the chart, and your boat must be somewhere along it. If you manage to establish a position line from one of many sources, you will have narrowed down the odds on your position quite considerably, and if nothing else you will know that there are many areas of the chart where you cannot be. A position line could be many miles long but knowing that you are somewhere along it is much better than knowing only that your position is somewhere in many square miles of ocean.

Most types of position line are straight but if it is derived from soundings it could be a long meandering line. Position lines derived from soundings can be ambiguous because if the line extends around a shoal your position could lie to either side of the shoal. Unless you can relate what you are seeing on the sounder to a precise change in depth that only occurs along one particular line, using soundings as a position line should be done with caution. Straight position lines can be derived from a number of sources: a compass bearing, a transit bearing, the course line and possibly a regular ferry route. Some of these need to be used with caution (such as the idea of a ferry on a fixed route) and instead of just being a thin line, some position lines could be quite wide, or even a sector radiating out from a source point.

A bearing taken from a yacht, for instance, is likely to have a possible error of a few degrees to either side of the reading, so when you transfer it onto the chart it would be better to show it as a narrow sector rather as a single line. The same would go for using the course line as a position line because you are never precise about the heading. By contrast a transit bearing is very precise and unambiguous, so it can be shown as a single line.

When you have two position lines that cross at a reasonably open angle, you have a position fix, but the accuracy of that fix will only be as good as the accuracy of the position lines you are using. One reason for suggesting that you draw some lines as a sector rather than a single line is to give a visual idea of the accuracy and if two of these sectors cross then you end up with a diamond of position. This fix may not be precise but at least you know that you are somewhere inside the diamond. Even if you cannot fix the position by getting two lines that cross, a position line can be very valuable as it shows you where the yacht is not rather than precisely where it is. At least you are narrowing down the possibilities.

A FERRY OPERATING ON A FIXED ROUTE CAN GIVE YOU A USEFUL POSITION LINE BUT USE THIS WITH CAUTION BECAUSE THERE IS NO GUARANTEE THAT IT IS ON THE DIRECT ROUTE.

21 LOOKING AT ALTERNATIVES

We have already touched briefly on looking at alternatives in the section on preparation but the paper chart presents the perfect tool for contemplating alternative strategies to deal with the weather or other circumstances changing along the route. The increasingly violent motion associated with the onset of bad weather is no place for the reasonable and rational thinking necessary to consider the alternatives. This is the sort of study that is best done in harbour before you leave, and having some alternative courses and harbours already laid out on the chart can make decisions a lot easier when you are out at sea.

There are three main factors that could make you start to look for alternatives. Firstly, on a powerboat you could find that you are using more fuel than anticipated perhaps because of head winds and seas. An alternative harbour somewhere along your chosen route that you could enter for fuel would be a useful place to turn to. Apart from the courses necessary to get there, it helps to have a note of any tidal limitations, facilities and the availability of fuel at these alternative ports.

Secondly, deteriorating weather could lead to you getting worried about the conditions you might find in the entrance to your destination port. A strong onshore wind could make the entrance untenable or at least dangerous and that is the last thing you want at the end of a voyage in deteriorating conditions with rough seas or local fog. Either way, it is useful to be able to consider an alternative port.

Thirdly, you might encounter sea conditions that are much worse than you anticipated. The weather is an obvious factor here, but you may have under-estimated the effects of a wind-against-tide situation. Tacking is one solution here and can be used by both power and sail. It can be beneficial if the seas are directly ahead or astern – by altering the course the wavelength is effectively increased and the motion of the boat should become easier. Having a ready-made track that can be put over the chart showing the tacks can indicate how much you can safely go off course in either direction.

Another situation could be when you have missed a tidal gate or have simply been going slower than anticipated, so you could be faced with an adverse tide over the last stretches of the journey. If you think about the alternatives early enough you can ensure that you have a strategy to deal with the situation, ensuring that you arrive upwind and/or up tide of your destination.

The paper chart is a mine of information about various aspects of navigation and the above ideas could be added to it (as described in 19: Customising the chart). In this way you can have most of the information you might need at sea readily available and in a useable form.

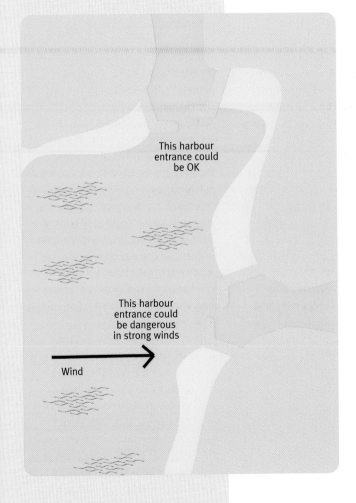

This harbour entrance could be OK

This harbour entrance could be dangerous in strong winds

Wind

22 USING DEPTH WHEN MAKING A LANDFALL

The depth of water under a boat is an important navigation tool even in these days of GPS. The soundings remain one of the quickest and easiest ways to confirm your position and there is a high level of reassurance in knowing that there is adequate water beneath the keel. One of the main criteria of navigating safely is to maintain enough depth of water under the boat to give a good margin of safety: whilst the chart should confirm the depth, the real-time readings from the sounder are a reassuring help.

The main time that a boat is at risk of grounding is when making a landfall or entering harbour, and this is where depth measurements can be a very important indicator. Even when the GPS shows the position to be safe, an adequate depth of water showing under the keel on the sounder is the important confirmation that you need. When navigating, an independent check is always important and this is one of the most useful roles of the sounder.

In order to use the sounder readings in a meaningful way you need to study the chart carefully, not only at the expected landfall point but also for a distance to either side of it. When the depth drops away quickly from the coastline you will get less warning that

you are approaching and a sudden shoaling on the sounder could mean that you are virtually on top it. By contrast a gradual decrease in the depth will indicate the approach to land with adequate warning.

The gradual shoaling appears to give the best results but because it is gradual there won't be a point at which you can say precisely that the boat is on a definite sounding position line or that you are a precise distance off because the decrease is so gradual. Then, when you see the shoaling, you cannot assume that you are making your landfall at the precise point that you were aiming for. This is why you need to study the depths on either side of the landfall point. This study may show that the depths are too irregular to give any meaningful indication of the distance off, or it could show that there should be gradual shoaling (so if the sounder shows a sudden shoaling, you are probably off course).

The value of using soundings when making a landfall will depend on each case and you have to make that judgement. It is easy to jump to conclusions and make the sounding appear to fit what you expect to see, but remember that it can get deeper again after it has started to shoal. Also, soundings won't necessarily be useful when making a landfall on a rocky coastline, particularly when there are off-lying rocks, because here you can find very sudden changes of depth and there may be little or no warning of a rock's proximity. The chart has to be your guide when using soundings and do not take too much for granted.

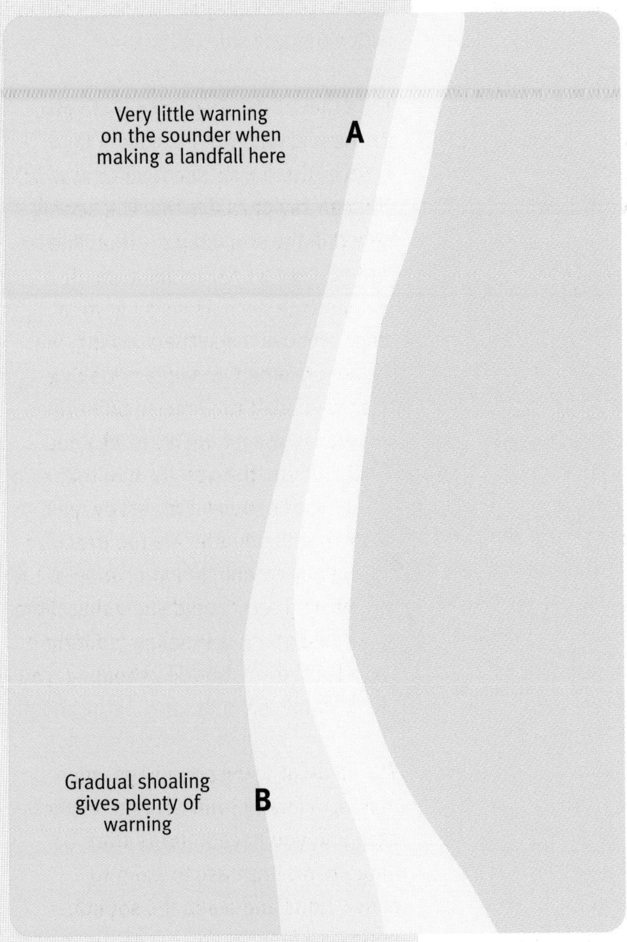

Very little warning
on the sounder when
making a landfall here

A

Gradual shoaling
gives plenty of
warning

B

23 DEPTH WARNINGS AND SHOALS

In the previous chapter we looked at how soundings can produce a useful guide when making a landfall, but they are also useful in general navigation. The fact that the depth shown on the sounder corresponds to the position shown on the chart is always reassuring and provides a good check, but soundings can also give you a more positive position check. Just like hills and features on land, the underwater areas also contain significant features that provide strong clues about your position.

When you have laid out your course line on the chart, whether it is paper or electronic, part of the checking process should be to identify significant changes in depth along the route. If you run your sounder at these points, the changes in depth that you see on the sounder are a useful position check. The tendency is to focus on shoals, because they tend to stand out on the chart, but troughs in the sea bed can be equally valuable as a position check. The main factor you are looking for is that the change in depth is relatively steep, so it's clearly visible on the sounder. A gradually changing depth will give a much less precise indication of your position even if it is still a clue.

The shape of a shoal will also have a bearing on the position-checking possibilities. A long shoal orientated with its long axis in line with your course will be more useful for checking that you are on course rather than the distance travelled. If you don't pick up this shoal on the sounder, you know your position must lie to one side or the other. When the shoal lies across your track you can get a check on the distance that you have travelled along the course (and there is also a position check as you cross each side of the shoal). Crossing a trough in the sea bed can give the same indications.

When you use this technique for position checking, you will not be so concerned with the actual depth that is shown on the sounder but with the change in depth. If you want to use actual depths you will obviously need to apply the height of the tide to the readings shown on the chart to get a true comparison. Using soundings in this way is unlikely to give you a precise position check but it will give you a position line along the side of the shoal, and you must be somewhere along it. You have to make sure that the position cannot be ambiguous, as there might be similar underwater features close by that could be confusing.

Another instance where soundings can give a valuable check is when running along the edge of a deep-water channel just outside the buoys (as you might do to avoid the big ships when entering harbour). Here the soundings can give a warning that you are moving too close to the edge, but do remember that some channels will have a very steep edge, with sudden shoaling, so there may not be much warning!

THE BREAKING WAVES ON THE FAR SIDE OF THE BEACON ARE A CLEAR INDICATION OF SHALLOW WATER.

24 DEPTH AND DISTANCE OFF

THE DEPTH OF WATER CAN OFTEN GIVE A GOOD IDEA OF YOUR DISTANCE OFF A HEADLAND.

There are many situations where it's helpful to know the distance off a point on shore. When you come into anchorage you will often look at the chart and want to find a spot that is quite close inshore. On a passage you will often want to pass a particular distance off a headland, perhaps to avoid rocks inshore. Of course, radar and the electronic chart can give a quick answer to your distance off, but because the margins can be quite small you want

a check and the depth of the water is often a reliable guide. However, before using depth in this way, study the chart carefully to ensure that any depth reading is going to give a good indication of distance, and that there cannot be ambiguity (if you are not measuring the depth in the place you expected to be or think you are).

Not only can depth give you an idea of the distance off a shore, it can also give

DEPTH, TIDES AND CURRENTS

the reassurance that you cannot always get from distances on the radar or the chart. Your sounder shows a physical measurement of the depth of water under your keel and even if the electronic chart suggests that it should be different, the sounder measurement should take priority and act as a warning that things aren't working out as planned (or a reassurance that they are).

This sort of depth-related-to-distance-off measurement is only valid when the depths shown on the chart decrease in a gradual way. On a steep-to shoreline it may be too late before you see the sudden shoaling on the sounder which suggests you are too far inshore of

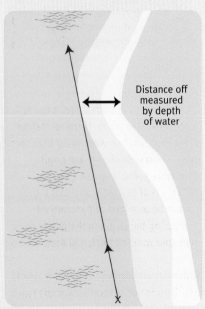

Distance off measured by depth of water

where you want to be. When rounding a headland, study the chart carefully and find a depth that corresponds to your required distance off. As long as the depth is greater than your 'warning' depth, you know you are on or outside your chosen track around the headland. A word of warning here – because the depths around a headland can often show considerable irregularities, there may be a shoal off the headland and then deeper water inshore of it. Your angle of approach could allow you to arrive in the deeper water inshore and miss the shoaling further out. You do need to look very carefully at the various possibilities.

Similarly, when coming into an anchorage, study the chart to find a depth that offers a reasonably safe distance offshore. Again, a steep-to shoreline is not the best situation in which to use this depth technique, but using soundings is very useful if you want to anchor really close inshore to find maximum shelter in severe conditions. You need to make sure that you are actually entering the anchorage at your chosen point by checking that the depths correspond to what is shown on the chart. Extra caution is needed here, because the surveys that are used to verify the chart information may not take place at regular intervals in waters off the normal routes.

25 THE EFFECT OF DEPTH ON SEA CONDITIONS

The fact that waves break in shallow water is well known, but there are two very different ways in which they actually break and this difference can be important if you are navigating in difficult conditions. Waves that are breaking onto a beach or on an exposed shoal are called translation waves. These rear up and dump their full weight of water into the beach or shoal, creating very fierce breaking waves. These are different to the waves that break over shoals or are caused by the effects of a wind-against-tide situation. Here the waves can break with what look like dangerous crests, but it tends to be only the crest that is toppling rather than the whole wave. Such waves are less dangerous to small craft, and there can be conditions where the depth is quite adequate for navigation but the relatively shallow water still produces nasty-looking sea conditions.

You probably see this to greatest effect in a harbour entrance where there is a bar. You know that there is adequate water in the entrance to get in across the bar but there appears to be an almost physical barrier in the way that the waves are breaking across it. Here, the waves become steeper and higher as they approach the shallow water and this becomes more noticeable when the tide is on the ebb and the wind is against the tide.

To a lesser extent you will see this same effect in areas where there is a transition from deeper to shallower water. Once the wave starts to 'smell' the bottom it will become higher and steeper. The relative closeness of the seabed also slows down the wave, and this in turn means that it will grow higher and steeper. When this sort of wave has a gradient of 18 degrees or more it will start to break, but it is only the crest that starts to topple, not the whole wave. Once the crest topples, the wave tends to stabilise again.

Where the edge of the shoal shelves very gently, the effect of breaking waves may not be so noticeable compared with a steep-to shoal where the sudden change in depth can lead to waves having a considerable change in appearance, possibly with breaking crests. Tides tend to be weaker over shoals (except in harbour entrances) but obviously if the wind is against the tide the change in wave appearance will be more noticeable (see 5: Judging sea conditions).

This change in the appearance of waves can serve as a useful indication and as a warning that you are entering shallower water. You may often see an area of breaking waves some way off, and this draws attention to the proximity of a shoal and so serves as a navigation warning. You have to treat this with a degree of caution because if you are viewing the waves from seaward and they are upwind, the breaking crests will not be so visible. It is the same when entering a harbour with a bar in an onshore wind - the waves will be breaking away from you and won't be so visible. In every case, breaking waves are more of a warning than a position check but they are still part of the repertoire of clues available to the navigator.

AS WAVES APPROACH SHALLOW WATER THEY WILL INCREASE IN HEIGHT AND THIS CAN BE A USEFUL GUIDE OR WARNING BEFORE BREAKING WAVES ARE ENCOUNTERED.

26 TAKING SHORT CUTS

It can be tempting when you look at the chart and see a short cut through shallow water that can save you a mile or two. The chart and the tide information shows that there should be enough water to make the passage but you ask yourself, 'If it is a viable channel, why Isn't It marked wIth buoys?' and 'In inshore waters like these where shipping does not normally venture, how reliable is the chart information?'

When it comes to the question of buoyed channels, you have to remember that channels tend to be marked with buoys to suit general traffic, which can include fishing boats and ships. Marking a channel with buoys is an expensive process and they are unlikely to be marked to suit small craft except where they may lead to a small port. Along the coastline it tends to be only off-lying shoals and rocks that get marked with buoys.

So, with your shallow draft, the passage in these unmarked inshore waters could be viable but then you wonder how reliable the chart information is. If the channel is not generally used by traffic it may not be surveyed as often as the main sections of the chart, so there is no doubt that using inshore, unmarked channels does incur an element of risk as sea bed features can change over

time and channels can move.

However, such channels are viable if you take care. The sea conditions might suggest that the water is too shallow for a safe passage (these warnings can be like those detailed in 25: The effect of depth on sea conditions). Although the changes in sea conditions can be a useful guide, you are going to get a much better indication of any unexpected shoals if there is a swell running in from seaward. Such a low swell is unlikely to impede your progress at sea but it's much more likely to generate breaking waves over the shallow patches of your route – these areas of breaking water can be a useful guide to the location of channels and a warning of any changes in the depths of water that might not be shown on the chart.

In adopting this method, it would be wise to operate at a slower speed which, of course, may take away any time saving that might be gained from taking the short cut. Sailboats should take the passage under power so that they can respond immediately to any dangerous shoaling. Always keep the sounder going because that can give you an early warning of shallows, and concentrate hard on all the signs and indications so you are ready to back off if you don't like what you see. Chart information is normally very reliable but shoals can move at short notice, particularly if there are strong tides and the sea bed is composed of sand. Passages with rocks may be less forgiving if you do touch bottom but they are unlikely to change over the years, so the chart information there should be more reliable.

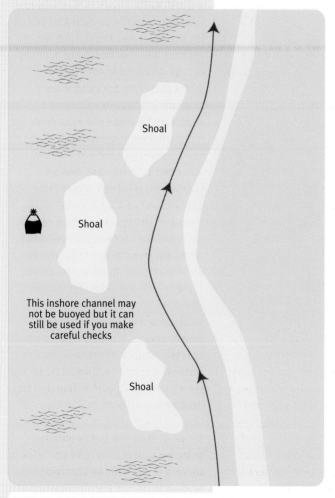

Shoal

Shoal

This inshore channel may not be buoyed but it can still be used if you make careful checks

Shoal

UNMARKED INSHORE CHANNELS MAY BE A VIABLE ALTERNATIVE BUT YOU WILL NEED TO CONCENTRATE AND KEEP THE SOUNDER RUNNING IF YOU USE THEM. ALWAYS BE READY TO STOP.

27 DISTANCE ON THE ELECTRONIC CHART

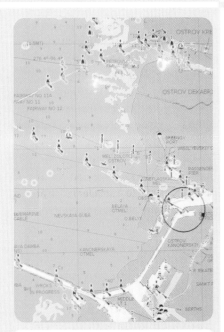

THE SCALE OF THE DISPLAYED CHART IS SHOWN IN THE TOP LEFT HAND CORNER AS 12 MILES AND THIS IS CONFIRMED BY THE LATITUDE GRID. FROM THIS IT IS POSSIBLE TO ROUGHLY ESTIMATE THAT THE WIDTH OF THE SHIPPING LANE SHOWN IS JUST OVER FOUR MILES.

If you want to measure distance on the paper chart, it's easy – you just use a pair of dividers to measure the chart distance and use the latitude scale at the side of the chart to translate that into actual miles. On the electronic chart, measuring distances is not so straightforward and without a realistic scale to judge things by it is much harder to see at a glance what the distance is off the land or other features.

When you just want to get a rough idea of a distance on the electronic chart, many of the displays have a small line in the top bar of the information screen with a distance alongside it. This is the scale but because you cannot transfer it to the chart you just have to try and visualise it by eye. Another option is to use the customising menu in the software to make the latitude and longitude grid appear on the chart display. This enables you to work out the distance between the latitude lines and translate into distance in the normal way, and gives you a better idea of scale, but it is far from an ideal solution.

A more positive measurement of distance can be made with the cursor. If you set it on the point you want to measure to, it will give a read out of the distance and bearing from where you are. However, this only allows you to measure the distance from where your boat is at the time to the point of interest. You cannot measure remote distances, such as setting a course and seeing how far it passes off a headland.

Range rings on the electronic chart would be a great idea but as far as is known the only way you can get these is to superimpose the radar display on top of the chart and to use the radar range rings.

When navigating with an electronic chart it's important to make sure that it is set to an appropriate scale. Using the right scale is equally important when planning a route on the chart because the scale of the chart dictates the level of navigation information that is shown. In order to avoid congestion on the chart, paper charts can be quite selective about the level of information shown on different scales, but even on large scale charts there will always be some indication of the smaller navigation features. Electronic charts are generally more selective about the level of information shown than paper charts, mainly because of the small size of the display. To avoid a saturated display, many features will be left out on the large scale electronic charts.

The difference between the paper and electronic charts is that whilst the paper charts may be selective, all the important features for route planning are retained. The selective process for electronic charts is less discriminating and you can find that important features like sectors on a lighthouse light and even buoys and shoal areas can be missing on the large scale, so you do need to change to a smaller range at intervals to ensure that you aren't missing anything of importance along the route.

When route planning, by all means set the basic courses on the larger scale charts for simplicity, but when you have done that, switch to smaller scales and check to make sure nothing has been missed along the way.

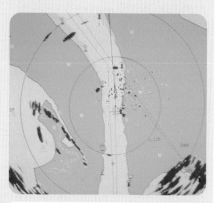

SEA CLUTTER SEEN HERE IN THE SPECKLED RETURNS NEAR THE CENTRE OF THE DISPLAY CAN MAKE IT DIFFICULT TO PICK OUT BUOYS AND SMALL CRAFT IN ROUGH SEAS.

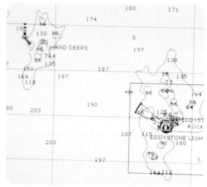

ON THIS 3-MILE SCALE THE HAND DEEPS BUOY IS MARKED BUT IT MAY NOT BE SHOWN ON THE 6 OR 12-MILE RANGE THAT YOU USE FOR ROUTE PLANNING.

29 GPS ACCURACY

Position accuracy is still at the heart of navigation, and modern GPS offers an unprecedented level of accuracy that is very difficult to argue with. On many electronic chart displays the accuracy is shown to four decimal places of a minute, which means that according to the display the accuracy is being measured to the nearest few inches. But just because the display shows the position to this level of accuracy doesn't mean that it exists. Certainly with the type of GPS receiver in general use for small craft navigation the accuracy will be much less, which should make you question just how accurate GPS is and how much you can rely on it. After all, the way you navigate and the margins of safety that you build in will depend considerably on the position accuracy that is available to you.

The type of GPS found on most yachts should be accurate to within 20 metres or so, and that level of accuracy should be more than adequate for general navigation. In fact, you won't normally work to that level of accuracy, but you might just want to when entering harbour in fog. Working to close navigation limits like this is fine provided that you take into account outside influences such as wind and tides and provided that you have some checks on position such as sighting buoys and using your sounder. If you do work to these close accuracy limits, you won't have any safety margins left so you need to get it right.

If you are going to work to the sort of accuracy that is possible with a modern GPS receiver, also bear in mind that the position shown on the display is the position of the GPS antenna. If the antenna is located at the stern then the bow of the boat could be many metres away from the actual position displayed.

Using buoys in conjunction with GPS positions can cause problems, because the location of a buoy is unlikely to be as precise as the GPS position. The buoys are likely to have been positioned using GPS but the position shown on the chart is the position of the mooring of the buoy on the sea bed and the buoy itself will move due to the slack in the chain that allows for the rise and fall of the tide. This is particularly the case in deeper water where there is more chain and at low water when there is more slack in the chain.

Another point to consider is the accuracy of the chart used to plot positions. Most modern charts, both paper and electronic, are now referenced to WGS 84, which is the datum now in general use on a worldwide basis. WGS 84 is compatible with GPS and is the datum to which the GPS positions are referenced, but where older charts are being used they could well be referenced to other datums and that will produce errors. If you have a different datum on the chart, most GPS receivers give you the option of changing the reference datum.

Finally, in poor visibility don't aim directly for the position of a buoy but preferably for a point some distance away. Heading directly for the buoy could put you in conflict with other yachts who are doing the same thing and it could get crowded close around the buoy as everyone exploits the accuracy of GPS to hit the same waypoint.

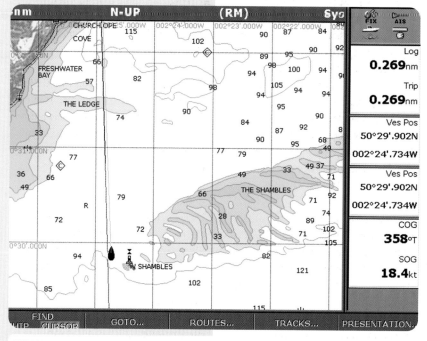

THE POSITION DISPLAYS ON THE RIGHT SHOW THE POSITION TO AN ACCURACY OF THREE DECIMAL PLACES, WHICH IS 1/1000 OF A MINUTE OR SIX FEET. THE GPS ACCURACY IS UNLIKELY TO BE BETTER THAN TWO DECIMAL PLACES OR 60 FEET.

30 KNOWING WHERE YOU ARE

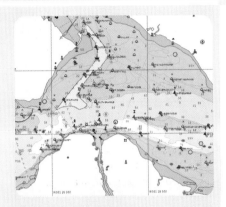

One of the significant changes that has taken place in navigation since the advent of GPS is that instead of focusing on where you are, the tendency now is to focus on where you are going. Position fixing is now so easy and available that you can concentrate your navigation energy on where you are heading. On the electronic chart the main instrument for doing this is the heading marker on the chart display. This is a significant navigation tool that allows you to line up the heading with your destination or the next waypoint, but to use it successfully it's important to understand how the heading reference is derived.

The normal heading marker shown on the display is calculated from historical positions. The last few positions derived by GPS are averaged out and the course made good over the ground is calculated from this and shown as the heading marker. Because of its historical associations this system will always have a slight delay in the heading marker responding to course changes. The accuracy of such a heading marker also depends on the accuracy of the GPS positions so it's likely that you will see short-term variations in the heading shown even when you are on a steady course. If you plan to line up the heading marker with your destination on the chart, you need to watch it for a short while and mentally average the heading.

The alternative type of heading marker is essentially a GPS compass. Using extremely clever software this system measures the Doppler effect (the change in frequency of the GPS signals caused by the relative movement of the satellite and the vessel) and from this, calculates the heading. The accuracy is around one degree, and although it doesn't work when the boat is stopped, that isn't a serious handicap. This type of heading marker gives the heading in real time, works well and is a great help in making real-time navigation plans.

Another type of modern heading reference is a true GPS compass. This has two GPS antennae mounted a fixed distance apart and the relative positions of the two antennae can be compared with a high degree of accuracy to produce a heading. This calculated heading is then applied to the electronic chart heading marker. Whilst this system has high accuracy it is also expensive and is less likely to be found on small craft.

When navigating with the heading marker you can line it up so that it shows you passing close to a buoy, a desired distance off a headland or towards a harbour entrance. This type of lining up could be more specific if there was a way of measuring the distance off from the heading marker at the distant point (as detailed in 27: Distance on the electronic chart). The result is that it gives you the true course to steer to your chosen point and this can be a useful technique for short-term navigation or for times when you need to change your plans when at sea.

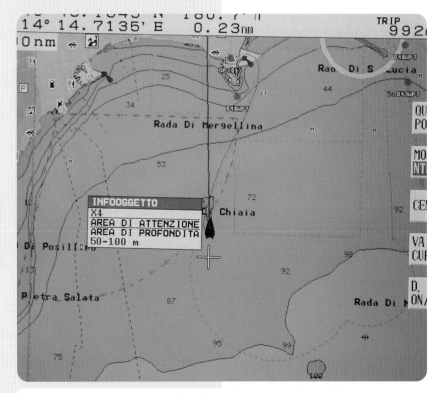

THE HEADING MARKER IN RED GIVES A CLEAR INDICATION OF WHERE THE VESSEL IS HEADING BUT YOU NEED TO KNOW ON WHAT THE HEADING INFORMATION IS BASED BEFORE YOU USE THIS FOR NAVIGATION.

31 WAYPOINT SELECTION AND USE

PICKING THE CORRECT WAYPOINT CAN HELP YOU FIND YOUR WAY INTO HARBOUR.

Waypoints are an essential part of electronic navigation and they are used to define the points along a route where there is an alteration of course. Because these waypoints are the turning marks along the route it is important that you choose them with care and check them again after the route is plotted. The course you will follow will link the waypoints, so after you have defined the initial plot, check along the proposed course to ensure that it offers a clear and safe navigation route.

Even with visual navigation, there were still waypoints. A waypoint is any point on the chart that you choose as a point at the end of a course. There was a time in the early days of electronic navigation that there were tables of waypoints listed by latitude and longitude so that

you could enter them into the electronic systems. Today it's much easier to select an electronic waypoint – you just pinpoint the spot with the cursor and the electronics do the rest. Because it's now so easy to select a waypoint in this way, it is also easy to be casual about it, but you should think carefully about where you place your turning marks, particularly if you are navigating in fog.

Waypoints are likely to be in two main locations: off headlands that are turning points in the route or at buoys that may mark dangers and also turning points along the route. When defining a waypoint off a headland you will need to think about what is a safe distance off to pass around the headland and this will be mainly dictated by dangers such as rocks or shoals that lie off the headland.

Much will also depend on the shape of the headland – it can often be necessary to place two waypoints at points around the headland to ensure a smooth passage. Also check out the possibility of tide races around the headland that may dictate whether you pass close in or a few miles out to sea.

When the waypoint is at a buoy try not to use the actual position of the buoy as the waypoint, even in clear visibility. Many other vessels may be doing the same thing and you could find yourself in congested waters. Passing a short distance off is not likely to add much to your route but you are likely to find clear waters there and you will also be allowing a safety margin (see 7: Safety margins). You might also want to modify your waypoints to meet other criteria (as mentioned in the Visual Navigation section) and to build in a margin for possible tidal flows in towards the land.

Setting a waypoint at your destination harbour will be part of the planning and you might want to build in an offset to the course to ensure that you arrive at the up-tide side of the harbour and don't have to fight the tide to reach the entrance. Selecting waypoints is the key to safe navigation whether you are navigating visually or electronically, and you need to take special care to get them right. It's not just the selection of the waypoint, but also what lies along the course in between.

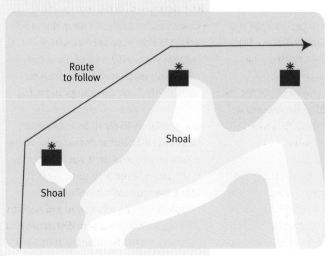

Route to follow

Shoal

Shoal

THE ROUTE IS PLOTTED OUTSIDE THE BUOYS TO ALLOW A SAFETY MARGIN.

32 WHEN YOUR GPS GOES DOWN

Although you may have GPS on board, if you are a serious navigator you will be keeping a separate plot on a paper chart and checking things out with visual clues as you make progress along the track. This means that if your GPS or the electronic chart system goes down you will still know where you are and where to go. However, it's very easy not to take this precaution and probably over 99% of the time you'll get away with it. One of the benefits of modern electronics is their excellent reliability, so you tend not to take precautions against failure.

There are three main possibilities of failure, the first being that the GPS system itself stops working, but this is a very rare situation. Secondly, the integrated electronic chart system on which you depend for the GPS position and chart information could fail. If this happens you not only lose the position information but also the chart display. Thirdly, there is the possibility of electrical failure in the circuits that supply the chart display.

In the first case, if you stop receiving positions from the GPS a warning will flash up on the display. Some electronic chart systems will continue to plot the track using dead reckoning based on the last course and speed, and that should at least get you near enough to your destination so that visual navigation can

IF THE GPS AND CHART PLOTTER GO DOWN BECAUSE OF AN ELECTRICAL OR ELECTRONIC FAILURE THEN HAVING A PORTABLE BATTERY OPERATED GPS ON BOARD CAN BE A GREAT HELP.

take over. In this situation it's important to maintain the same course and speed (and the possibility of failure is one good reason to set the autopilot manually rather that integrate it directly with the chart system). At least then you will have the course to steer to your destination. With the coming availability of an alternative satellite positioning system called Galileo there could be the possibility of an alternative.

If the chart system goes down through an internal fault, you won't have access to any position or chart information. If you are a conscientious navigator you will have jotted positions down in your log book so that you will have a reference position available for future navigation. In this situation you still want to maintain the course and speed but now you will need to pay much more attention to possible visual clues. If you also have a paper chart available it shouldn't be too difficult to navigate to your destination.

In a worst-case scenario with no paper chart and no course to steer, you should at least know the direction of the land, so you can head there and watch for visual clues. The depth sounder is vital here, and the possibility of GPS failure is a good reason for not having the sounder integrated into the chart system. You can always get direction clues from the wind and the sun

provided that you have been taking note of these when the GPS was working. Many of the visual navigation techniques from this book should also help. If the cause of the breakdown is in the electric supply then it may be possible to restore this.

The best solution to guard against possible failures is to have a portable GPS plotter available, together with a supply of batteries. In this way you are not reliant on the boat's electrical supply and you have an independent backup for the main plotter. Any failure of the GPS signals themselves is likely to be temporary and when Galileo arrives there will be a backup for the satellites as well.

A GPS FAILURE CLOSE TO LAND SHOULD NOT BE A PROBLEM BUT IN THE OPEN SEA IT CAN BE CHALLENGING.

With everything you use for navigation it is important to know the level of accuracy that you are being presented with, so you know how much you can trust the information. So often an electronic display looks very positive and accurate and it's hard to argue or negotiate with it. You will rarely find any of these electronic displays giving any indication of the level of accuracy that you can expect and radar is no exception. You don't get a position in latitude and longitude from radar unless it is integrated with the chart plotter, and the only independent way to establish any sort of position from the radar is to use a range and bearing from a known object on the display, or two or more ranges from fixed objects.

Range on the radar is very accurate, at least for practical purposes. The only qualification here is that the target you are measuring from may not be too

clearly defined. Buoys and rocks may give a sharp image and a positive point to measure from but if the land is defined by a shelving beach then the position of this will vary with the tide and you cannot be exactly sure which point of land you are actually measuring from. However, if you can clearly identify the targets that you are measuring from, fixing the position from ranges on the radar should give a positive position.

Bearings do not have the same level of accuracy. If you are operating the radar in relative mode, that is, with the boat's head at the top of the display, then all bearings that you take from the display will be relative to the boat's heading. If you want to get a compass or a true bearing from this information, you will need to apply the boat's heading to the

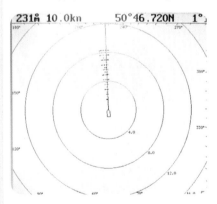

THE RANGE RINGS ON A RADAR ARE ALWAYS GOING TO BE MORE ACCURATE FOR POSITION FIXING THAN A BEARING, PARTICULARLY WHEN THE RADAR IS OPERATING IN RELATIVE MODE.

relative bearing in order to get a bearing you can use on the paper chart.

If you are operating the radar in North Up mode the boat's heading will be automatically applied to the radar, and depending on whether the heading is compass or true any bearings taken from the radar can be used directly on the paper chart. Most users are reluctant to use a North Up display on the radar because it does tend to swing around as the compass heading changes but you would only need to use this format when comparing the radar display with the electronic chart or when having a radar overlay on the chart. In any situation where the boat's heading is automatically applied to the radar you do need to be aware of whether this is a magnetic or true heading and any bearings taken from the radar will need to be considered in the same way. In relative mode the boat's head will vary with steering alterations so unless you take the boat's heading at the time you take the bearing, errors will creep in.

When you use radar to fix the position, try to stick with ranges. Bearings come into their own when the radar is being used for collision avoidance tactics because you are then more interested in the relative location of the other vessel.

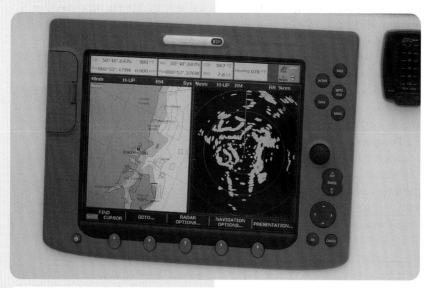

WHEN NAVIGATING WITH RADAR, THE RANGE WILL ALWAYS BE MORE RELIABLE THAN A BEARING.

34 ROUNDING A HEADLAND ON RADAR

RADAR RANGES CAN BE A GREAT HELP WHEN ROUNDING A HEADLAND.

Rounding a headland is always a significant event on a coastal passage and it can be greatly assisted by using radar. You can set waypoints off the headland and use the electronic chart plot to work your way round but headlands come in a wide variety of shapes and sizes, with many headlands extending for several miles, and this is where radar comes in useful.

Rather than getting round the headland by following a series of waypoints, work out the minimum distance off that provides you with a safe passage. Now you can use the variable range marker on the radar to present a warning ring for the distance that you are off the land. If the land returns on the radar, come within this pre-set range and you'll know it's time to head out and increase the distance off.

Headlands are often places where you find stronger tides and/or currents with localised flows that can set you in towards the land. This means that this technique can be particularly beneficial for slower yachts, which are more affected by these uncertain tidal streams (which can cause the yacht to experience an unexpected set). The radar can also be useful if you are planning to take an inshore route around the headland that might take you inside some off-lying shoals or rocks. Here you need to establish a precise distance off and the radar can be a great help for this.

Some radars incorporate an anchor watch facility that will warn a vessel if it is dragging its anchor. To enable this, you establish a pre-set range on the radar and it gives a warning if the yacht moves away from this range. Using this to round a headland can give you an audible warning if the yacht comes within a prescribed distance of the land and this can be an added safeguard.

Measuring the range off is only one use of radar when rounding a headland. The waters off a headland are usually the areas where you find the strongest tides – in these strong tides you can often find areas of breaking waves as the tides are accelerated and diverted around the headland. In daylight, you should be

RADAR FOR NAVIGATION

able to spot these breaking waves in time to take avoiding action but at night these visual sightings are not possible.

This is where the radar comes in because these breaking waves will usually show up on the radar display as regions of expanded sea clutter in a localized area. The breaking waves can present quite a distinctive target on the screen, particularly if you are heading into the wind and the waves are breaking towards you. To enhance the possibility of detection in this way make sure that the sea clutter control is set to maximise the wave returns so that they are not subdued and lost. Detecting the breaking waves in this way on the radar can be useful if you are planning to take an inside passage around the headland that can often be clear of the breaking waves out to seaward.

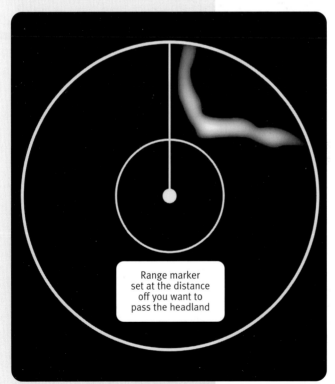

Range marker set at the distance off you want to pass the headland

THE RANGE MARKER ON THE RADAR CAN BE A VALUABLE AID TO ENSURE YOU PASS A SAFE DISTANCE OFF WHEN ROUNDING A HEADLAND.

35 RADAR OVERLAYS

The two main electronic displays available for the navigator are the radar and the electronic chart. They both use different systems to produce navigation information and neither of them on their own provides the most comprehensive picture that you need. Combine the two and you have the best available electronic information but there are two alternative ways to do this.

Provided that they both have the same orientation (normally North Up) having the radar and the electronic chart displays side by side can enable a direct comparison. Having the radar picture overlaid on top of the chart display is the other option – there can be considerable benefits with this because the two sources of navigation information are complimentary.

The ability to overlay the radar picture onto the electronic chart is a feature of many modern electronic systems and it can be used to advantage in some situations. The radar will show targets that are ships and boats, which is something the electronic chart cannot do. It will also show buoys and land features, and here it compliments the information shown by the electronic chart. The electronic chart will display all the fixed navigation information but not the moveable features like ships and boats. This means that where radar

targets correspond with features shown on the electronic chart, they can be assumed to be navigation features, but whilst when they don't correspond with features on the chart, they can normally be assumed to be vessels either moving or at anchor.

One benefit of having the two displays combined is that it can allow you to positively identify the land features that are showing up on the radar. This can be useful when making a landfall, as the radar may pick up returns from higher ground inland before detecting a foreshore that is low-lying.

This discrimination in identifying vessel targets and land features by direct comparison can be particularly useful in poor visibility, but having the two combined like this can lead to a saturated display in crowded waters. There can be just too many targets on the combined screen for you to get a clear picture of what's going on. You may also want to have the chart and radar displays on different ranges for navigation purposes (perhaps looking further ahead on the chart than on the radar) so having the radar overlay on the chart may not always be the best option.

Having the radar overlay on the electronic chart, and the synergy between the two, does enhance the level of information available. The chart shows the underwater features (something the radar can't do) and the radar shows other vessels, which is something the chart can't show. Combine the two and you have a more complete electronic picture of what's going on around you. How and when you use this is largely a matter of personal preference and is likely to be determined by the particular navigation situation. You may be able to get similar results by having the radar and the chart displays close alongside each other whilst still retaining a clearer picture on each display.

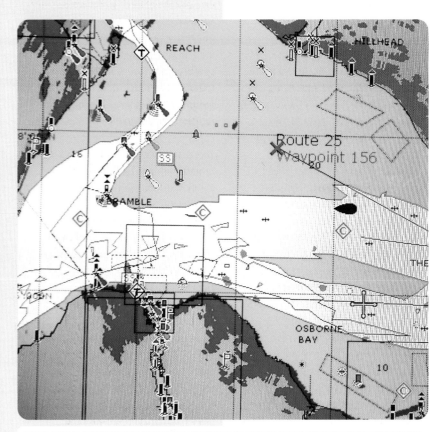

HAVING A RADAR OVERLAY ON THE CHART (DARK BLUE ABOVE) CAN BE A HELP WHEN DIFFERENTIATING BETWEEN BUOY AND VESSEL TARGETS.

36 WHAT THE RADAR CANNOT SEE

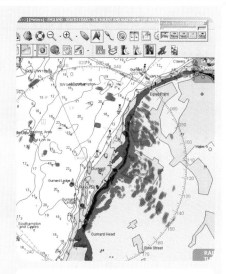

THIS RADAR OVERLAY CLEARLY SHOWS THE AREAS WHERE THE RADAR CANNOT 'SEE' SUCH AS THE HARBOUR IN THE TOP RIGHT CORNER.

Radar does not have the precision that is found in most other electronic navigation systems and there are several limitations to what it can tell you. There are also limitations in how it displays information and it is important to understand these if you are to use the radar safely. These limitations mainly involve things that the radar cannot see or cannot differentiate between.

Part of the problem with radar (and one that can cause difficulty in understanding for new users) is that whilst the display is shown as a plan of the area around you, rather like an aerial view, it actually looks at targets with a horizontal view, just as you might looking around the horizon. Radar has a horizontal beam that travels outwards from the antenna and is then reflected back from any dense object that it comes into contact with. This means that smaller ships could be hidden behind a larger one or a buoy target might not show up when you expect it.

The radar beam cannot see through solid objects because the beam is reflected from these and does not penetrate any further. For instance, if the radar antenna is set low and you stand in front of it there will be a gap on your radar display where the radar cannot see through you. Although this is given as an example it can actually be a problem on some flybridge motor yachts and can lead to the assumption that there is nothing ahead when in fact the radar beam is being blocked so that it cannot see ahead. It isn't hard to imagine the consequences of this when you are entering harbour and think the radar is showing a clear run ahead.

The radar cannot see around corners either. You won't see anything on the far side of a headland until you are well round it and the next bay opens up to the radar beam. On a twisting river you will have limited visibility around the bends and in many harbours there can be blank areas. In most cases, the radar picture will become clearer as you get closer.

Another problem with many small boat radars is that the radar beam has a wide horizontal angle, maybe up to four degrees. This means that any targets within this four-degree sector at the same range will appear as one target and won't separate out. Things will tend to become clearer as you get closer, and this should take some of the confusion out of the situation when using radar for collision avoidance. It is the wide beam angle that also explains why a narrow

harbour entrance channel may not always show up clearly as a marked channel until you get closer. From a distance the buoys on each side will tend to merge into one and there may not be an apparent gap between entrance piers until you get close.

The vertical beam angle of the radar is usually around 25 degrees, so in heavy rolling seas or when a sailboat is well heeled over in a breeze to more than 12 degrees, you could loose the picture at the sides. The problems with sea clutter are dealt with separately in 39: Lost in the clutter.

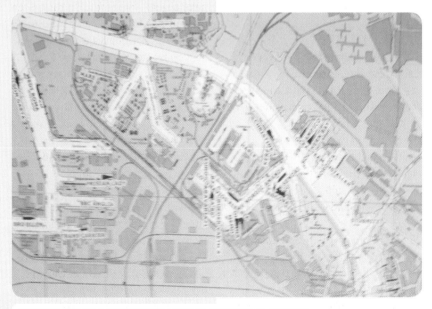

AIS TARGETS CAN LOCATE SHIPS (SHOWN IN DARK BLUE) THAT THE RADAR CANNOT SEE.

37 CHANGE OF BEARING

If the bearing of an approaching vessel is changing significantly, there is no risk of collision. That seems a pretty straightforward rule to avoid collisions at sea but it does need qualification. Firstly regarding how you check whether or not the bearing is changing and secondly, what constitutes a significant change in the bearing?

In good visibility you can monitor the change simply by watching the approaching vessel and you will soon know whether the change is significant when you can visually see it. However, it is important that your boat maintains a fairly steady heading when you are looking at the bearing because the change of bearing is a relative measurement. If the boat's heading changes, so will the apparent bearing of the other vessel, but that's not the change of bearing that you're looking for. This is a good reason to run on autopilot, as it makes it much easier to establish any change in bearing. You can measure the bearing with a hand-bearing compass, but the visual check is usually adequate because you are looking for a significant change.

That significant change should be at least ten degrees over a period of a few minutes. However, if the other vessel is approaching from nearly ahead then you won't see much change until the last

minute. You will be able to see by the angle of approach of the other vessel whether or not it is going to pass clear but there is unlikely to be any significant change in bearing until the two vessels are quite close.

The problem of measuring the change of bearing can become more acute when using radar for collision avoidance. On the radar display you can put the bearing cursor on the target that you are watching and look for a significant change in the bearing. Here it is assumed that you are using the radar on a relative display with the boat's head pointing to the top of the display. Again, an approach from ahead will not show much change and it's best to assume the possibility of collision and alter to starboard just in case. If you have the display on North Up the change in bearing will still be relevant for collision avoidance.

In any case of doubt about the change of bearing, assume that a risk of collision exists and make an early alteration of course if it is your job to give way according to the Colregs. If you are the stand-on vessel then monitor the situation carefully and be prepared to take avoiding action if a close quarters situation develops where the two vessels are within one mile of each other. If you do make any alteration of course to avoid a collision then this should be 20 degrees or more so that the other vessel is left in no doubt about your intentions. Also, watch for any alterations by the other vessel because this could affect your planned avoidance tactics. You can also slow down to buy yourself more time. Bear in mind that we are only talking about coping with a single vessel in a collision situation but you may have to deal with several at one time in busy waters – here the slowing down tactic will allow you more time to sort things out.

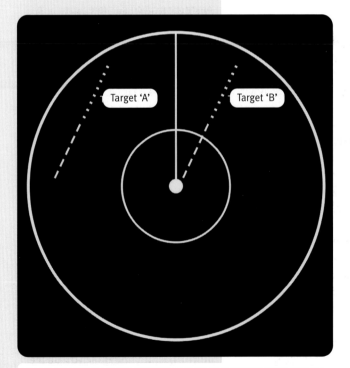

Target 'A'   Target 'B'

THE PLOT OF TARGET A SHOWS THAT IT WILL PASS WELL CLEAR WHILST THE PLOT OF **B** SHOWS THAT IT IS ON A COLLISION COURSE AND ACTION NEEDS TO BE TAKEN.

38 WHICH RADAR SCALE TO USE

When you are using the radar, whether for navigation or collision avoidance, it is important to have the display on the correct scale. If you are operating in the sort of poor visibility where radar becomes the priority navigation tool, the scales required for these two functions may not always be compatible and the collision avoidance requirements should take priority because the electronic chart can cope with most of your navigation requirements.

The scale that you use in poor visibility will also depend on the speed of your craft. For a sailboat operating at, say, six knots under power, the three-mile range is probably best to use when the visibility drops below one mile. For a faster craft such as a powerboat running at around 20 knots, the six-mile range might be more appropriate. On the three-mile range when running at six knots you should have 30 minutes between detecting a target at the edge of the display and the collision point. At 20 knots you would have a time of 18 minutes from first detecting the target if you were operating on the six-mile range, always assuming that you can detect the target at that range.

In either case there should be ample time to keep track of the target and to see if its bearing is changing significantly. The speed at which you operate will of course depend on the range of visibility. A visibility of one mile will seem quite adequate for most small craft to operate at their full speed but at half a mile you should start to think about reducing speed. A lot will depend on the circumstances but in crowded waters where there is a lot of traffic you might want to buy more time by reducing speed early.

One of the best solutions for using radar in poor visibility is to have a double radar display, where it's possible to display two alternative ranges on the same screen. This gives you the option of having one display on, say, the six-mile range to give early warning of approaching craft and for use in general navigation, and the other on the three-mile range for the actual collision avoidance manoeuvres. These double displays are available but they don't come cheap so you will probably need to compromise. One alternative solution is to switch between the three and six-mile ranges to keep a check on what's approaching from a distance and to get a better feel for what is going on around you whilst still having the shorter range to give you a clearer picture of the collision risks.

In crowded waters you might want to use an even smaller scale, perhaps between one and two miles, because you can only handle so much information on the radar display. To simplify the collision avoidance task you can then focus on those targets that appear to pose the main collision threat – mainly those ahead and on the starboard side, where it is your job to give way. Also, slowing down will buy you more time to assess a developing situation. Whatever you do, it's still vital to keep a good visual lookout to avoid nasty surprises.

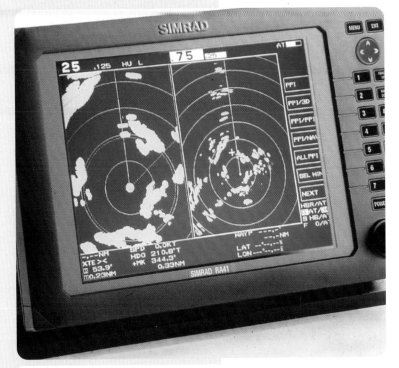

HAVING A RADAR DISPLAY THAT CAN SHOW TWO DIFFERENT RANGES AT THE SAME TIME CAN BE A GREAT HELP IN POOR VISIBILITY.

39 LOST IN THE CLUTTER

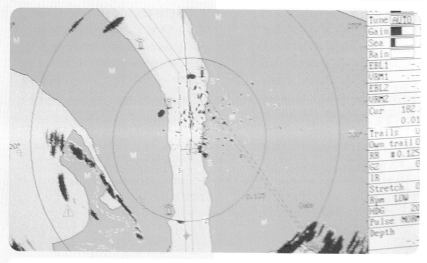

SEA CLUTTER, SEEN HERE IN THE SPECKLED RETURNS NEAR THE CENTRE OF THE DISPLAY, CAN MAKE IT DIFFICULT TO PICK OUT BUOYS AND SMALL CRAFT IN ROUGH SEAS.

So-called 'clutter' on the radar screen is caused primarily by the radar beam being reflected by the waves on the surface of the sea. The rougher the sea, the bigger the waves, and the greater the extent of the clutter on the radar display. In a strong blow you could get clutter extending up to two miles or so from the centre of the display. The sea clutter seen on the radar screen will rarely be regular all round the centre of the screen because the waves that lie to windward of you are likely to generate more clutter than those down to leeward. The reason for this is that the waves to windward will present a steeper face to the radar beam than those to leeward.

You can reduce this clutter by using the sea clutter control but this effectively reduces the strength of the radar returns on a graduating basis extending out from the centre. It doesn't just reduce the strength of the returns from the waves, but from any radar target that might lie within the range of effectiveness of the clutter control effect. As far as the radar display goes it seems like a good idea to reduce the apparently superfluous clutter from the centre of the display but in doing so you are also reducing the ability of the radar to detect small craft within the same area because they produce a relatively weak radar return, similar to or only marginally stronger than the radar return

74

from waves. The only difference between the radar returns from small craft and those from waves is that the wave returns are generally random and inconsistent whilst the boat returns will be continuous. Sophisticated radars use this difference to help identify the small craft amongst the waves but the average small craft radar does not have this facility.

Of course, this same problem means that other craft may not be able to see your yacht on radar in rough seas. Even big ship radars can suffer from this problem and there is a real possibility that your yacht won't be detected on their radar. The only real solution to this problem is to make your yacht more radar visible and the various means of doing this are given in 41: See and be seen. These should help, but you cannot rely on other yachts around you having one of these devices, so they may not be radar visible. You can assume that there is a good chance that radar will detect the other craft, but they can get lost in the clutter. It is perhaps fortunate that rough seas and poor visibility don't tend to occur together, so when you really need to detect other craft there is a reasonable chance that you will see them on radar, but a good visual lookout and moderate speed are still vital to ensure safety in poor visibility.

BECAUSE OF THE SEA CLUTTER, THIS BOAT IS UNLIKELY TO SHOW ON THE RADAR.

40 AVOIDING THE BIG SHIPS

KEEPING OUTSIDE THE MAIN CHANNELS CAN HELP TO AVOID BIG SHIPS.

There is a degree of incompatibility between big ships and small craft and this is not just a question of size. The big ships have very different manoeuvring characteristics from small craft and the views from their helm stations can be very different. In fog, a small craft will almost certainly see a big ship on its radar but there is no guarantee that the reverse will be true. So when it comes to collision avoidance in poor visibility, it becomes a lot easier if you can rule the big ships out of the equation.

Avoiding smaller craft tends to be easier because they are likely to have similar handling characteristics to your own yacht, but it's a different matter with shipping. Firstly, you cannot always be sure that they have seen you, particularly at night or in fog, and secondly, they may not always give way according to the Colregs either because there's no depth of water to allow them to manoeuvre around you or because they assume that you will keep out of their way because you are smaller. Ships

COLLISION AVOIDANCE

tend to rely a lot more heavily on their radar for collision avoidance (and they have more sophisticated radar for this) but it doesn't offer any guarantee that they will see you.

There is one simple way to avoid the big ships and that is to keep in the areas of shallow water where they cannot navigate. Big ships will tend to stay at least a mile or more offshore around headlands, so if you stay inside that you should be OK. In harbour entrances the buoys marking the channels are normally set to mark the deep water required for shipping rather than a channel for shallow draft yachts, so you will generally find that there is adequate water for a yacht outside the buoyed channel.

In open waters there are now many areas where the ships have to keep to the defined one-way shipping routes that are marked on the chart. These traffic lanes are mandatory for all craft over 20 metres in length so larger yachts may have no choice except to mix with the general shipping, but at least it will all be travelling in the same direction. For smaller craft, staying outside these lanes will help you to avoid the ships, but you cannot guarantee there won't be any as ships can deviate outside the mandatory shipping channels if they are making for harbour entrances. If your

route does take you into or across these shipping channels then make sure you cross them at right angles to get across as quickly as possible (and also to meet your obligations under the Colregs).

Before adopting these avoidance tactics do study the chart carefully to ensure that the proposed route is safe. For example, sometimes the buoyed channel designed for shipping can be very close to shallow water where the shoal has a steep edge after dredging. Although you can never be sure that you will avoid all the ships by using these techniques, these tactics will at least reduce the chances of encounters of the wrong kind.

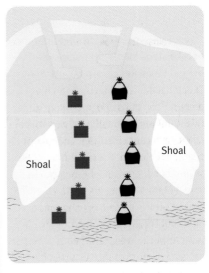

KEEPING JUST OUTSIDE THE BOUYED CHANNEL WILL KEEP YOU OUT OF THE WAY OF BIG SHIPS.

41 SEE AND BE SEEN

One of the basic requirements for collision avoidance is for the two craft involved to be able to see each other. Obviously a visual sighting is the best type of 'sighting' and a radar sighting can be a good substitute, but you cannot take any realistic action until that initial sighting has been made. This can present a problem for small craft because they're not the easiest things to 'see' at sea.

To make a visual sighting, the first requirement is to have a clear view outside. Apart from smaller open boats, nearly every craft (sail and power) has blind spots that can be caused by sails, masts, windscreen pillars or even just salt spray or reflections on a windscreen. It's important to realise where blind spots are on your boat and to take steps to see what might lie behind them. Regular small alterations of the course can often be enough to open up any blind spots and this is most important at night where pinpricks of light can be hard to see at the best of times. Foresails that extend right down to deck level can present a particular problem for sailboat vision and the only real solution here is to go out on deck and look around the sail.

So much for being able to see other vessels – you also want to be seen by them. Good, bright navigation lights make your vessel easier to detect – whilst you may think that your lights look bright from a close view, try and get them assessed by someone a mile away. At that distance they may look more like glow worms than proper navigation lights. This problem of being seen can be vitally important as far as shipping is concerned and you want the brightest lights possible, no matter what the regulations require. The wide separation of the lights on a sailboat under power can be particularly confusing to other craft.

In terms of radar visibility, the antenna has to have a clear view around the horizon. People standing in a boat, particularly on the flybridge of a powerboat, can obstruct the radar beam and create a gap in the picture that looks apparently clear of targets. Sails can also reduce the strength of the radar signals passing through them and lead to a deterioration in the radar sensitivity.

In terms of being seen by other radars, a radar reflector can make your boat a better radar target and a Radar Target Enhancer (RTE) is even better. Best of all is a Search And Rescue Transponder (SART), which is an active transponder that is triggered by the radar beam of other vessels. These are primarily designed to aid liferaft detection in an emergency but you might want to think of switching yours on in busy shipping lanes. An AIS receiver can give longer-range identification but it only works if both of the vessels involved are suitably equipped.

Whilst you may think that your boat is highly visible, try to imagine what it will look like from other vessels. That is what really counts, and your supposedly bright lights may be just pinpricks from a distance, particularly on a sailboat without any white lights. Remember that small craft can easily be lost in the sea clutter on the radar of another vessel and in rough seas even navigation lights could be lost in this way. Never assume that the other vessel has seen you just because you can see it.

PEOPLE STANDING ON THE FLYBRIDGE COULD BLOCK THE VIEW OF THE RADAR IN THE FORWARD SECTOR JUST WHERE YOU NEED THE BEST RADAR PICTURE IN POOR VISIBILITY.

42 RUNNING ON AUTOPILOT

Running at night or in fog can put your navigation under considerable pressure. You are trying to steer a course, keep a lookout, perhaps trying to count the flashes of the light on a buoy, and do the navigation, all at the same time. It may be possible to share this workload between crewmembers but even then things can get difficult, and in these conditions it is usually the vital lookout that suffers. However, you can take the steering job out of the equation by switching on the autopilot. This is the traditional claim of the autopilot manufacturers and there is no doubt about the immediate benefits to your workload, but using the autopilot can have many other benefits that are worth considering.

Take that flashing buoy light for instance. Because you are under pressure when hand steering and your concentration is distracted, the course being steered is likely to be erratic. Wandering off course by 20 degrees or more would be quite normal in this situation, which means that that buoy light will never be in the same place when you look for it again. As you search the horizon trying to find it you are neglecting other vital jobs. Switch on the autopilot and the buoy light should come up on more or less the same bearing each time you look for it, and you can relax a bit. It will be the

same for the lights of other vessels around you, and you'll be able to keep a better check on their progress and possible threat. They are also more likely to have a better appreciation of your movements if you maintain a steady autopilot course.

One of the main benefits of the steady course generated by an autopilot will be seen when using the radar. Most small boat radars operate on a relative motion basis, which means that any change in heading will change the orientation of the radar display. If your yacht's heading is swinging through 20 or 30 degrees, the blip of an approaching boat will swing around on the screen by the same amount, which makes it much harder to interpret the radar display and check on the bearing of the approaching vessel. In fog this swinging around of the radar display can present serious difficulties, particularly when using the radar for collision avoidance.

Using an autopilot on a sailboat brings even more advantages, the main one being that the sails will work much more efficiently on a steady course, assuming that you have a steady wind. You won't have the sails flapping when you lose concentration on your steering and you will be much more in control of the situation. You can also minimise the risk of a broach.

There is a natural reluctance to use an autopilot in difficult situations, particularly fog, because you may need to make an instant alteration of course when something looms up ahead. One weakness with many modern autopilots is that the disconnect button that allows you to take over hand steering can easily be lost amongst the rest of the controls on the unit, particularly at night. When you are buying an autopilot, try to get one with a prominent disconnect button and a rotary knob for course control rather than one that uses push buttons.

USING THE AUTOPILOT FOR STEERING AT NIGHT OR IN POOR VISIBILITY CAN BE A GREAT HELP. THIS TYPE, WITH A ROTARY COURSE CONTROL KNOB IS THE BEST FOR COURSE CONTROL.

43 SPEED IN THE FOG

With modern electronic navigation techniques there is a greater temptation to think that you don't have to restrict your speed so much in poor visibility. With radar it's easy to assume that you can 'see' all of the other vessels around you and as the electronic chart shows you where you are, why worry? The problems can start with small craft that may not show on radar or be lost in the sea clutter. 39: Lost in the clutter, shows how this can be a problem not only for you detecting other craft but also for them 'seeing' you on radar. You can never be 100% sure that you can see everything that's out there, so in most fog situations you must use reduced speed. The Colregs also demand this and it pays to remind yourself just what they do say on the subject.

With the good manoeuvrability of most small craft it's easy to assume that you can quickly avoid anything that comes out of the fog ahead. However, you first have to see the other craft visually, which means keeping a constant lookout. If you are keeping a good lookout visually, can you also monitor the radar adequately? Reduced speed is the only sensible answer.

Because the unexpected can and often does happen in poor visibility your speed should be such that you can stop before you hit something. That is essentially what the Colregs say, and you may think that this means being able to come to a stop within the limits of the visibility, but you are assuming that the other vessel isn't moving. If the other vessel is travelling towards you then you will meet somewhere in the middle of the range of visibility before you are both stopped. This means that in order to be safe, your speed should be such that you are able to stop within half the limit of the visibility. Of course, you also have your steering control to help take avoiding action but you also need to build in a margin for the time it actually takes to detect the other vessel visually and that could be well under the range of visibility.

When you are working out the safe speed for poor visibility you tend to assume that you are keeping a good visual lookout and this is a vital requirement in fog no matter what electronics you are using. You also assume that you are ready to stop, so a sailboat should be under motor in these conditions. Alterations are an alternative to stopping but they usually take more time because you first have to assess what the other vessel is doing. There's no substitute for being able to stop and it's your responsibility to make sure you can. Take the time to check out your stopping distance in clear weather using the GPS – you could be in for a surprise when you see how long it can take.

IN FOG YOUR SPEED SHOULD ENABLE YOU TO STOP IN HALF THE DISTANCE OF THE VISIBILITY.

44 REFLECTIONS AND VISIBILITY

Being able to see from the helm is a vital requirement for safe navigation and it's particularly important at night or in poor visibility. This sounds obvious but it is surprising how many yachts, both motor and sail, only have limited visibility. Being out in the open greatly increases the visibility from the helm (and sailboats have the edge here) but often the sails, mast and rigging can impair the view ahead. It's important to know what limits, if any, the sails are making to the visibility so that you can take steps to mitigate the effect. Another problem at night can be light reflections from stainless steel rails and rigging, and on powerboats the masthead light is often located where it lights up half the foredeck.

On powerboats there are a surprising number of areas where the visibility might be poor and this can particularly apply to the view astern. It is arrogant to assume that you are going faster than other craft on the water and that you need not bother with the view astern.

The flybridge on a motorboat should offer good visibility in all directions and this is the place to be when you are navigating in fog or at night when you need the clearest possible view of your surroundings. If the flybridge is not available or tenable, be aware of how the visibility can be limited from the wheelhouse. Wide windscreen pillars can cut off quite a sector of the view, sometimes over an arc of 15 to 20 degrees, and they are certainly wide enough to hide the lights of a ship if it is some distance away. Reflections of lights from the dashboard, or from the saloon behind, that appear on the windscreen can also make it harder to see lights outside and they will distract your attention from the view. These reflections will be particularly bad if the windscreen is tinted.

Lights and screens in the wheelhouse or at the helm can also divert your attention from the outside view. The radar and electronic chart displays can usually be switched into a night mode to reduce the glare from the screens but these displays also present another visibility hazard. At night and in fog, these displays will nearly always present a much more interesting picture than the view out through the windscreen, and the temptation to look at the displays rather than the outside world is very strong. There may not be anything to see and focus on outside, whilst the displays keep you up to date with the constantly changing navigation scenario. In an ideal world the displays would be separated from the outside view so they don't conflict, but the best that can be done in most cases is to be aware of the limitations of the outside view and try to compensate for them.

One of the better ways to avoid all these visibility problems is to station one of the crew outside where there is a good view (at least over the ahead sector) so that their only role is to keep a lookout. That way you can compensate for the inadequacies of most helm positions but make sure there is verbal communication between the lookout and the helm.

THICK WINDSCREEN PILLARS AND REFLECTIONS ON THE GLASS CAN REDUCE VISIBILITY FROM THE HELM CONSIDERABLY. SAILBOATS NEED TO BE AWARE OF SAILS OBSTRUCTING VISIBILITY, PARTICULARLY AT NIGHT.

45 FINDING A BUOY IN FOG

FINDING A FAIRWAY BUOY CAN BE A CHALLENGE IN FOG.

We have shown various ways that enable you to know which way to turn or what to do when making a landfall in poor visibility but the most difficult thing of all is to find a buoy in fog. This is the ultimate navigation challenge because you do not usually have any kind of reference (such as the land or shoaling water) as a guide. Of course, if you have a working GPS it shouldn't be too difficult to find the buoy and if you only have a short distance to run from the last fix, you should be able to steer an accurate course and see the buoy. The problems start when you have steered the required course and covered the required distance by timing, and nothing shows up. That means you're not where you expected to be and you have to take steps to locate the buoy and get back on track.

When heading for a buoy you could offset the course to be sure you are to one side or the other of it, and then you will at least know which way to turn to find it. However, this technique doesn't work very well because it means that you are going to miss the buoy anyway and finding it eventually will depend on how accurately you have measured the elapsed distance.

There are better techniques, and you should set a course directly for the buoy in the hope of hitting it spot on. If it does not show up as expected the next step is to run a bit further on the same course, just in case your calculation of the speed or of the tides was not accurate. If there's still nothing at this stage there is a great temptation to start wandering about aimlessly in the hope that you'll spot something. That is a sure way to get lost and the best solution is to start a square search.

This is the same as the search used when rescue craft are trying to find a casualty. First of all, estimate the distance that you can see and use this to govern the dimensions of the search. After you have gone past the buoy turn at right angles to your course and run the visual distance that you have estimated. Turn at right angles again so that you are reversing the original course and run twice the visual distance. Then turn at right angles again in the same direction and run three times the visual distance. If you keep this pattern going, increasing the distance at each

turn, you will go round in a series of ever increasing squares, but covering all the area within a visual range. This way, you should pick up the buoy you are looking for.

There are a few points to watch here. Firstly and most importantly, keep a lookout at the sides as well as ahead, because it is more likely you will see the buoy somewhere on the beam than ahead. Secondly, a buoy usually marks a shoal or danger of some kind, so bias your search to seaward rather than inshore where the danger might lie. Thirdly, keep the sounder running as a check that you're not getting too close to the shoal.

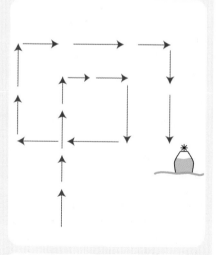

A SQUARE SEARCH TO FIND A BUOY.

FINDING A BUOY IN POOR VISIBILITY CAN BE A GREAT RELIEF.

46 ASSESSING HARBOUR ENTRANCES

When making plans for a passage, you will have a destination harbour in mind. The weather conditions may look set fair; will they be OK for entering your chosen destination harbour? Whilst many (or perhaps most) harbours don't have much in the way of weather restrictions for entry, give some thought as to what the conditions might be like in the entrance and whether you will be able to use the chosen harbour on arrival.

In the context of making an easy passage you may well want to take what looks like the good option of running downwind. When the wind is behind you on the passage, it will be blowing straight into your destination harbour. Although many harbours can be entered safely in a fresh onshore wind, you might want to consider what the conditions will be like if your chosen harbour has a shallow bar across the entrance. Here, you could be faced with breaking seas when there is a fresh breeze blowing.

In many harbour entrances, the sea conditions are likely to be worse if there is a strong ebb tide running out of the harbour. The sea conditions around a harbour can deteriorate quite dramatically, even when there isn't a bar across the entrance channel. You might also experience difficult conditions when

the entrance is guarded by breakwater that drops vertically into the sea. This can cause a confusion of reflected waves off the vertical stone walls and the resulting clapotic seas can be extremely difficult to cope with in a small boat. Be aware that you could find quite severe local conditions when the wind is blowing into the harbour; just what you don't need at the end of a day's sailing.

IT CAN BE VERY DIFFICULT TO ASSESS WHAT THE CONDITIONS MIGHT BE LIKE IN A HARBOUR ENTRANCE WHEN VIEWED FROM SEAWARD AND IT CAN PAY TO GET ADVICE FROM THE SHORE IF POSSIBLE.

The main requirements for an anchorage are: shelter from the wind and the waves, the absence of any ground swell that can cause uncomfortable rolling, and a good holding ground so that there is minimum risk of the anchor dragging.

Shelter from the wind and sea looks pretty straightforward and in theory, if you tuck yourself in under the land, there should be all the shelter you want. However, if the land around the anchorage is high and perhaps mountainous, in a strong blow you can get serious squalls running down off the mountains, even though you are on their lee side. The squalls seem to accelerate down the mountain slopes – you can often see them rushing across the water whipping up a white spray, and they make life very uncomfortable.

The ground swell is much harder to escape from. The inshore end of the swell is slowed down first when it reaches a headland, and this slowing down means that the swell can swing round in direction and roll right into what looks like a good sheltered anchorage. You can expect to find this sort of ground swell when the wind is or has been quite fresh outside and it will continue even after the wind has dropped away. One way to avoid it is to find an anchorage where you can put shallow water between you and the direction from which the swell is coming from.

Good holding ground such as a sand or shingle bottom can be identified by looking at the chart, but don't expect to find this information in the same detail on the electronic chart.

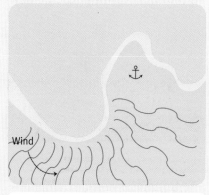

WAVES CAN BE REFRACTED AROUND A HEADLAND AND THIS MAKES IT VERY UNCOMFORTABLE IN THE ANCHORAGE, EVEN THOUGH IT SEEMS THAT IT SHOULD BE SHELTERED.

IT SHOULD BE SHELTERED INSIDE THAT OUTER BREAKWATER BUT THE SEAS ARE SWEEPING ROUND THE END AND MAKING THE OUTER SECTION UNTENABLE.

48 FINDING A HARBOUR ENTRANCE

ENTERING A HARBOUR IS ALWAYS A CHALLENGE FOR THE NAVIGATOR.

At night or in poor visibility it isn't always easy to find a harbour entrance. Even in good conditions, there are many harbours that have little in the way of distinguishing features when viewed from seaward and the situation can be more complicated at night. The buoys or other flashing lights that are used to indicate the channel or the entrance may not always show up against the shore lights, particularly if there are flashing neon lights in the vicinity. If you're using GPS, you can have some confidence that you are positioned off the harbour entrance but you still need to pick out those lights to get confirmation.

Radar offers one possibility of getting the reassurance you need and confirmation of where the channel lies but even on radar it can be difficult to identify a narrow entrance channel, and at many harbours there may be no distinctive radar features. You expect radar to produce the answer, and it probably will as you get closer, but many small boat radars have very poor discrimination and an entrance channel may not become clear until you get quite near.

The reason for this is that the width of the radar beam can be as wide as four degrees. This means that two or more targets at the same range within that four-degree sector will show up as a single target. Buoys marking a channel leading into the harbour may not show up as a clear channel and could look instead like a single line of buoys. The entrance breakwaters, perhaps sticking just a short way out from the land, may not show as an open entrance. Just when you want a nice clear picture of the harbour entrance, all you get is a confused display that may not relate to what the paper or the electronic chart is telling you.

The radar picture can become more confused if there are breaking waves on shoals near the entrance. With an onshore wind, there may even be breaking waves across the entrance that show up on the radar and make the picture more confusing. You could be as close as two miles or less before the picture on the radar starts to become clearer. Shipping in the entrance could also confuse the picture.

The best solution is to use the electronic chart to make the approach. This won't show a confused picture (provided that the display is set to a suitable scale) and you should get an unambiguous presentation of the approach. Making a harbour approach like this could be a very good time to have the radar picture superimposed over the electronic chart. In this way you will be able to relate what the radar is showing to what the chart shows, and get a double check. The redeeming feature of making an approach with electronics is that the closer you get, the clearer the picture should become, but you have to be prepared to deal with the intricacies of the harbour channels. Preparation is important here, particularly when a flood tide is carrying you into harbour, and it's less easy to stop and work things out if you're not sure. This is a good time to have the sounder on as well.

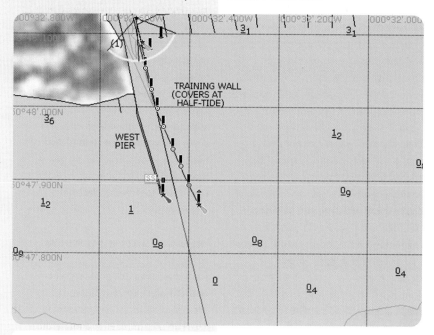

THIS HARBOUR ENTRANCE LOOKS EASY TO FIND ON THE CHART BUT IT MAY NOT SHOW UP CLEARLY EITHER ON RADAR OR VISUALLY UNTIL YOU ARE QUITE CLOSE.

49 ELECTRONIC CHARTS FOR HARBOUR NAVIGATION

In theory you should be able to navigate safely into a harbour just using the visual signs of buoys and other marks. This is what the marks are there for and they are what the pilots who are bringing the shipping in and out will mainly be using. Any dangers in or near the entrance channel are usually clearly marked and your main concern might be with the depth of water if the tide is low. However, coming into a strange harbour is not always as easy as the chart might suggest. The chart gives you a plan view of the layout but you are looking at the same scene with a horizontal view from the helm. What looks clear and obvious on the chart can be confusing from the helm because the various features you are looking at are superimposed one behind the other.

The electronic chart can be a great help here because it not only shows your position quite precisely in relation to the features that you see in front of you, but the display can also show alternative views. Part of the latest technology in electronic charts enables you to replace or supplement the normal plan view of the conventional chart with an actual aerial view. This photographic view can be a great help in building up a mental picture of what the area actually looks like. The best time to do this is before you enter the

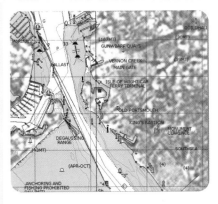

ENTERING HARBOUR CAN LOOK STRAIGHTFORWARD WHEN SEEN ON THE ELECTRONIC CHART BUT YOUR VIEW CAN BE QUITE LIMITED AS YOU COME IN AND THE GPS MAY NOT BE ACCURATE ENOUGH FOR CLOSE QUARTERS NAVIGATION.

harbour, so that during the actual entry things will hopefully have a more familiar look.

Three-dimensional views are also available with many of the modern electronic chart systems but they tend to be more concerned with underwater features than those above ground. Using some of the alternative viewpoints of the harbour during the time you are actually making the entrance is not recommended because it can tend to take your focus away from the conventional chart plot, and that still remains the vital plot that you need to confirm your position.

The horizontal view from the helm may still be confusing, even with all this help from photographic information. The secret here is to focus on the more immediate surroundings and to try and identify those whilst ignoring the more distant features. At the same time, it helps to keep a constant check on the electronic chart because that will show your position at all times. See also 50: Entering a harbour at night.

When you call up the display of a harbour on the electronic chart system it is always surprising to see just how much detail is shown. In theory, with this level of detail, you should be able to navigate right into a harbour by using the electronic chart but the position accuracy of the GPS (see 29: GPS Accuracy) should make you adopt this approach with caution. The use of the electronic chart should be as a guide rather than the only navigation method, and there is no real substitute for visual information when you are entering harbour. The key to success is in being able to translate what you see on the chart into what you expect to see around you.

THE ELECTRONIC CHART SHOULD ONLY BE A GUIDE – THERE IS NO SUBSTITUTE FOR VISUAL INFORMATION WHEN ENTERING HARBOUR.

50 ENTERING A HARBOUR AT NIGHT

AT NIGHT THE LIGHTS OF SHIPS CAN BE CONFUSED WITH SHORE LIGHTS, AND EVEN FLASHING NAVIGATION LIGHTS CAN BE DIFFICULT TO PICK OUT.

Entering harbour at night can be a challenging experience even when the harbour is relatively familiar. The main problem stems from the difficulty in picking up the navigation lights that are there to guide you in, but identifying the harbour features can also create difficulties. Even in the harbour approaches it can be hard to identify the navigation lights against the background of shore lights and flashing neon signs, and shipping movements and other craft can add to the confusion.

The first step in entering a harbour at night is preparation. Study the chart carefully and in detail so that you build up a mental picture of what it might look like. As seen previously, many electronic chart systems allow you to see an actual picture of the harbour but of course these are daylight pictures so they may not be so helpful for night entry. Making a list of the various flashing lights that you might encounter in the harbour should be part of your preparation work, and if you are using a paper chart then you can mark these clearly on the chart.

Tidal information will also be important. If you have a choice, enter harbour against the ebb tide so that you can stop and work things out when you're not sure. Although entering on a flood tide does give you the benefit of a rising tide if you should touch bottom, the ebb tide is best because your planning should keep you well clear of any potentially dangerous shallows.

It is in these difficult night time circumstances that the electronic chart really comes into its own. The modern cartography used in these charts displays the harbour features in considerable detail and you should be able to rely on the GPS position shown on the electronic chart to an accuracy of 20 to 30 metres, which should be enough to enable you to cope with the main parts of the entrance work. The heading marker will be a vital part of this because it shows you where you are heading, which can often be more important that your actual position.

Be aware that in a steep-sided harbour you could suffer a temporary loss of GPS positioning if the satellites are obstructed from a clear view of your antenna. This means that the electronic chart positioning should be used as a guide rather than the primary means of navigation, which must remain the visual one.

One of the major problems in entering a harbour at night is in identifying other vessels that may be moving in the harbour. The fixed lights of these vessels won't always show up well against the shore lights, particularly when the vessels are slow moving or at anchor, and the masthead-mounted white lights on sailboats operating under power can be particularly difficult to see. Radar set on a short range could be helpful here, particularly in picking out shipping in the harbour.

THINGS CAN LOOK VERY DIFFERENT AT NIGHT.

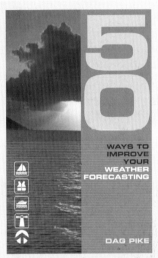

50 Ways to Improve Your Weather Forecasting
Dag Pike
ISBN 978-0-7136-8268-7

Weather forecasts often leave out a lot of useful detail, and the timing of changes can also be vague. Dag Pike shows you how to translate the basic information into really practical forecasts – sailors will be able to make better use of the available wind and avoid difficult areas, whilst powerboat drivers will be able to find the smoothest waters for a better ride. Packed with expert tips, this book is your passport to practical weather forecasting.

Dag Pike is one of the most experienced seamen in the world and is the author of several books and many articles for leading nautical magazines.

50 Ways to Improve Your Powerboat Driving
Dag Pike
ISBN 978-0-7136-8269-4

This is a book about practical powerboat driving in boats large and small, and contains techniques that can only be picked up from experience – practical ways to make your driving safer, easier and better, whatever the conditions.

Dag Pike gives advice on handling a fast boat in waves and head seas, matching response times to sea conditions and using the throttle to affect trim. You may have learnt the important basics of powerboat driving, but now it's time to translate these into practical handling techniques to give a better ride and a smoother passage.